D1521759

PRIESTHOOD AND DIACONATE

GERHARD LUDWIG MÜLLER

PRIESTHOOD AND DIACONATE

The Recipient of the Sacrament of Holy Orders
from the Perspective of
Creation Theology and Christology

Translated by Michael J. Miller

IGNATIUS PRESS   SAN FRANCISCO

Title of the German original:
Priestertum und Diakonat
Der Empfänger des Weihesakramentes
in schöpfungstheologischer und christologischer Perspektive
© 2000 Johannes Verlag, Einsiedeln, Freiburg

Cover art Christopher J. Pelicano
Cover design by Roxanne Mei Lum

ISBN 0-89870-892-3
Library of Congress Control Number 2001094786
Printed in the United States of America ∞

CONTENTS

CONTENTS 9

FOREWORD

The greatest challenge facing the Church in Europe and North America is to find a new and credible way to proclaim the gospel. Do we as Christians bear witness to our faith in Jesus Christ, and do we live it in such fashion that he "can show man the way and strengthen him through the Spirit in order to be worthy of his destiny", that is, the supreme destiny of fellowship with the triune God? (Second Vatican Council, *Gaudium et spes* 10). The mystery of his existence becomes clear to man when by faith he recognizes that Jesus Christ, the Son of God, is the key, the center, and the purpose of all human history, and when he embraces this truth by a life of following Christ.

This must be the concern dearest to the heart of the Church and of every Christian, in the parishes and in the study of theology, especially at the threshold to the new millennium, when Christianity can look back with gratitude on the two thousand years of its history since God became man "for us and for our salvation". All of our efforts to proclaim the faith and to study it theologically ought to be consolidated with a view to this one theme.

Then again, there are the "provocative themes", which often demand all the attention and which, considered in and of themselves, are worthy of all sorts of theological investigation. The discussion about the possibility of ordaining women as priests and deacons has led the Anglican Communion into an endurance test. The Church's Magisterium has interpreted the tradition of the Catholic Church, which it shares with the Orthodox Churches and which was reiterated by Pope John Paul II in his apostolic letter *Ordinatio sacerdotalis* (1994), as a divinely revealed truth and a doctrine that binds in faith. This makes clear that the Church's practice in this regard cannot be interpreted as a concession to the customs of an age, for instance to a discrimination against women on sociological grounds. At the same time, however, theology must also take up the task of describing anew the active cooperation of women in the life and mission of the Church. It must do this against a twofold background: first, in light of an ecclesiology of *communio*, which goes beyond every clericalistic restriction of the concept of Church; and simultaneously with reference to a more profound anthropology, in the context of the social and cultural conditions in which women and men live, which have completely changed since the Industrial Revolution.

As a consultant to the Doctrinal Commission of the German Bishops Conference and as a member of the International Theological Commission, I have dealt on several occasions with questions about ordaining women to the priesthood or to the diaconate. Besides a few essays, these investigations resulted in two books, *Frauen in der Kirche* [Women in the Church] and *Der Empfänger des Weihesakraments* [The Recipient of the Sacrament of Holy Orders], both of which were published in 1999 by Echter Verlag, Würzburg.

In many reviews and also in personal conversations I was called on to collect in one volume these contributions to a systematic theology of the priesthood and the diaconate, thus making them more easily accessible. The contributions that are reprinted here have been revised and in part considerably expanded and updated.

I hope that a fair and free discussion of controversial

themes can help to overcome tensions within the Church. The purpose of this volume is to communicate a theological insight into and understanding for the causes and the intrinsic meaning of the Church's doctrine and practice. No one could ever accept a situation in which Christian women, who for two thousand years have been important collaborators in the Church's mission, found themselves restricted to a secondary role because of the Church's doctrine on the recipient of Holy Orders or felt that their dignity as women and human beings was being slighted.

We will again have a clear view of the calling that is common to all Christians and to their ordained shepherds. Being a Christian means being "consecrated to be a spiritual house and a holy priesthood" through the Sacraments of Baptism and Confirmation. That is why all men and women of the Church should "bear witness to Christ and give an answer to everyone who asks a reason for the hope of an eternal life which is theirs" (Second Vatican Council, *Lumen gentium* 10).

Munich, New Year's Day 2000,
Solemnity of Mary, the Mother of God

Gerhard Ludwig Müller

ABBREVIATIONS

The Documents of the Second Vatican Council

AG   *Ad gentes [divinitus]*. The Decree on the Church's Missionary Activity, December 7, 1965.

CD   *Christus Dominus*. The Decree on the Pastoral Office of Bishops in the Church, October 28, 1965.

DV   *Dei verbum*. The Dogmatic Constitution on Divine Revelation, November 18, 1965.

GS   *Gaudium et spes*. The Pastoral Constitution on the Church in the Modern World, December 7, 1965.

LG   *Lumen gentium*. The Dogmatic Constitution on the Church, November 21, 1964.

PO   *Presbyterorum ordinis*. The Decree on the Life and Ministry of Priests, December 7, 1965.

SC   *Sacrosanctum concilium*. The Constitution on the Sacred Liturgy, December 4, 1963.

Additional Abbreviations

AAS   *Acta Apostolicae Sedis*

BKV   *Bibliothek der Kirchenväter* [Library of the Church Fathers], second series

Cath   *Catholica: Vierteljahresschrift für Ökumenische Theologie* (Münster)

CCC   *Catechism of the Catholic Church*, 1993

CCEO   *Codex Canonum Ecclesiarum Orientalium*

CIC   *Codex Iuris Canonici*

COD   *Conciliorum oecumenicorum decreta*, ed. G. Alberigo et al. 3d ed. Bologna, 1973

CSEL   *Corpus scriptorum ecclesiasticorum latinorum*, Vienna

DACL   *Dictionnaire d'archéologie chrétienne et de liturgie*, Paris

DH   H. Denzinger, *Enchiridion symbolorum, definitionum et declarationum de rebus fidei et morum: Kompendium der Glaubensbekenntnisse und kirchlichen Lehrentscheidungen*, trans. and ed. [Latin-German] by P. Hünermann. 37th ed. Freiburg i. Br., 1991. [Cf. *The Church Teaches: Documents of the Church in English Translation*, trans. and ed. by John F. Clarkson et al. Rockford, Ill.: TAN Books and Publishers, 1973. The selections in this book were taken principally from the 24th, 28th, and 29th editions of Denzinger's *Enchiridion symbolorum*.]

DThC   *Dictionnaire de théologie catholique*, Paris

EstTrin   *Estudios Trinitarios* [Salamanca]

FC   *Formula Concordiae*

FThS   *Frankfurter Theologische Studien*

FZPhTh   *Freiburger Zeitschrift für Theologie und Philosophie,* Fribourg

HDG   *Handbuch der Dogmengeschichte*

HK   *Herder Korrespondenz*

HKG   *Handbuch der Kirchengeschichte*

IKaZ   *Internationale katholische Zeitschrift* (Communio [cf. English edition])

JbAC   *Jahrbuch für Antike und Christentum*

JThS   *The Journal of Theological Studies*, London

LJ   *Liturgisches Jahrbuch*

LThK   *Lexikon für Theologie und Kirche*, 3d series

LXX   Septuagint

MD   John Paul II, apostolic letter *Mulieris dignitatem*, August 15, 1988

MThZ   *Münchner Theologische Zeitschrift*

OS   John Paul II, apostolic letter *Ordinatio sacerdotalis*, May 22, 1994

PG   *Patrologia Graeca*

PL   *Patrologia Latina*

PLS   *Patrologia Latina, Supplementum*

SCh   *Sources Chrétiennes*

SCG   Thomas Aquinas, *Summa contra gentiles*

ST   Thomas Aquinas, *Summa theologiae*

ThHNT   *Theologisches Handwörterbuch zum Neuen Testament*

ThQ   *Theologische Quartalschrift*, Tübingen

ThWNT   *Theologisches Wörterbuch zum Neuen Testament*

TRE   *Theologische Realenzyklopädie*

TThZ   *Trierer Theologische Zeitschrift*

UTB   *Uni-Taschenbücher*

VApS   *Verlautbarungen des Apostolischen Stuhls* [Announcements of the Holy See, a vernacular periodical along the lines of *The Pope Speaks*]

I

A CHALLENGE FOR
CONTEMPORARY ECCLESIOLOGY

The expressions of appreciation, indeed of admiration, concerning the importance of women in society and in particular for the Church that Pope John Paul II included in his *Letter to Women* (1995) created a positive stir in the media. Yet it appeared to not a few commentators that the statements in this letter could not be reconciled with the 1994 magisterial declaration in *Ordinatio sacerdotalis* (= OS) that women are not called to the priesthood and with the determination "that the Church has no authority whatsoever to confer priestly ordination on women" (OS 4). Many suspected that behind the *Letter to Women* there was even an attempt to weaken the Church's position as a reaction to the scathing criticism that this magisterial decision evoked among the public in Europe and North America.

Ordinatio sacerdotalis seemed to confirm quite a few commonplace notions about the misogyny of the Catholic Church. In the view of outsiders, the "nonadmission" of women to "positions of leadership" hardened the prejudice with regard to the ingrained conservatism of religion and especially of the Catholic Church, which out of pure spite was cutting herself off from the trend toward a modern democratic society of equal rights and emancipation.

Accordingly many committed Christians also see in the "nonadmission of women to Holy Orders"—and in further dogmatic, disciplinary, and moral positions—the main reason why so many people have turned away from the Church, both interiorly and practically. "Stalled reforms" are preventing a new springtime from beginning. In all seriousness, though, even if this source of friction were removed, could we really expect to see a reversal of the trend toward secularization in society and a new encounter with the gospel? The Protestant and Anglican ecclesiastical communities that live in the very same historical and spiritual conditions as the Catholic Church in Europe and North America provide, *mutatis mutandis*, a test case.

This hope, though, which has not been confirmed in practice in the communities just mentioned, seems to have been linked to the so-called "*Kirchen-Volksbegehren*" ["Church-People's Petitions", affiliated with the "We Are Church" movement] in German-speaking lands in 1996–1997. Besides a call for the abolition of priestly celibacy, criticism of the indissolubility of marriage, and challenges to the restriction of sexuality to marital relations between a man and a woman, another main theme was the demand to admit women to *all* official positions, more precisely to the *Sacrament of Holy Orders*.

Some of these demands touch upon questions of faith, for instance the basic sacramental understanding of the Church. Then, too, the epistemological question is raised: Upon what foundations is the Church's profession of faith built, and on what interpretive authority does her faith-consciousness rely?

Every attentive observer notices the fault-lines, in some Western European countries at least, of a sort of intellectual division within the Church, which given suitable politico-social circumstances could also lead to a visible schism. Precisely when dealing with the theme of "Woman in the Church", an "atmosphere" laden with emotion manifests itself, which often leaves little room for open dialogue and objective argument. Someone who advocates a contrary thesis can scarcely count any more on being heard at all, much less hope that his arguments will be considered morally or intellectually tenable.

This difficult topic is connected with the equally fundamental discussion of the ecclesiological status of the priestly office. To be precise, it is a question of the relation between the common priesthood of all the faithful and the ministries of the bishop, the priest, and the deacon, which are based on the Sacrament of Holy Orders (LG 10); specifically, it is also a question of the ecclesiological place of lay people in the Church's apostolate of pastoral care, proclamation, and service (LG 33). A decisive factor for the Second Vatican Council was a comprehensive view of the Church as a *communio*. The Council's fundamental concept of the Church, which is based on a biblical and patristic understanding, seems however to have gone largely unnoticed. Instead of an internally coordinated multiplicity of specific services, ministries, and charisms within the common participation in the prophetic, priestly, and pastoral ministry of Jesus Christ, a *strategy of conflict* is again evident that makes its presence felt in a "battle for the places of honor".

The disputes about the *Instruction on Certain Questions about the Collaboration of the Laity in the Priestly Ministry* (August 15, 1997) have once more made clear that today there are *two* ecclesiologies, which no longer seem to be compatible with one another, under one organizational roof in the Catholic Church. Like different denominations, they are already mutually exclusive in their membership and their preoccupations. Will two different branches crystallize out from this unstable mixture of dissolved compounds, as in the case of the Anglican churches: one "high church" and the other more Protestant with a relatively functional understanding of ministry? Will an "official episcopal church" be in constant competition with a "lay church" consisting of "base communities"?

The reaction to *Ordinatio sacerdotalis* has precipitated a stereotypical pattern for evaluating magisterial documents, at least at the level of the mass media and of public opinion. The catchphrase of "democratizing" the Church seems to have become a pretext for making even doctrinal questions subject to majority rule. The correct theological insight, that we are a communion of people who believe in Christ and thus constitute *his* Church, seems to have been distorted into the notion that the Church is *our* property and that her profession of faith has to be fine-tuned each time with a view to attracting adherents, like a party platform at a convention of delegates.

Some academic theologians have subjected the Church's magisterial documents to a test of their theological validity by holding them up to their own subjective standard of plausibility as the ultimate criterion for what a magisterial statement can say. This subordination of the Church's tradition and the Magisterium to private theological blueprints reopens the debate about the fundamental concept of revelation and how it is made present in each generation in the faith of the Church. What is the relationship between the teaching authority of the bishops and the theological interpretation of Sacred Scripture and of the deposit of faith by individual theologians?

It goes without saying that authoritarian or egalitarian alternatives for a Church "from above" or "from below" cannot counteract an intellectual schism that already exists, no more than emotionally charged classifications of themes and individuals as "conservative" or "progressive" could. It is not a question of who stands his ground or proves his point at the end of the tug-of-war; rather it is a matter of recognizing what it is that revelation presents to man, to which he then opens and subjects himself in faith by the power of the Holy Spirit. Some orientation is provided here by theological epistemology, as it was developed as early as the second century (in the conflict over the Gnostic usurpation of Christian themes), when the criteria for theological knowledge were formulated as the principles of apostolic writings, apostolic tradition, and apostolic succession. These epistemological criteria for theology recently received again an authentic formulation at the Second Vatican Council in the Dogmatic Constitution on Divine Revelation, *Dei Verbum*, which is a fundamental presentation of how the revelation of the triune God is comprehended in and conveyed by Jesus Christ.

Precisely upon this foundation, a dialogue about these explosive contemporary issues again becomes possible and meaningful. A search for truth that is objectively oriented, together with trust that all who take part in the discussion are in earnest, is capable of counteracting a break-up of the ecclesial community.

Certainly the problem of women in the contemporary Church should not demand the same energy and attention as the question of whether human beings can believe in the existence, presence, and incarnation of God in the first place. All discussions about Holy Orders and about the valid recipient of the sacrament would prove to be vacuous if the profession of faith that Jesus is the Christ were no longer communicated so credibly and attractively to future generations that people could place their hope in him alone, whether in life or in death.

Under the heading of questions about God and the crisis of faith, though, falls the contemporary theological and anthropological task of establishing the fact that women *are* Church, of formulating anew their common and specific contribution to the "building up of the Church, which is the Body of Christ". There are conclusions to be drawn from this with regard to the concrete form that life in the Church takes, considering the crisis in belief about God. A prerequisite for this is the recognition—without any distorting prejudices—of the completely transformed context of technological civilization in the industrialized world and an assessment of the way in which men and women experience themselves, particularly in their relations with one another.

The statements on the anthropology of man and woman, as set forth so emphatically in *Mulieris dignitatem* (1988), and on the Church and the sacraments, especially Holy Orders and Matrimony, must be examined with a view to determining their fundamental dogmatic content and then inculturated in a creative way into the contemporary Western world and into other traditions as well.

This cannot be separated from a simultaneous critique of the ideological standards implicit in modern civilization's view of man in terms of "self-creation, self-realization, and self-glorification", which is incompatible with the Christian understanding of man in his relationship to God, who creates and perfects man. Accepting one's createdness and listening to the good news proclaimed to the poor proves to be a method of humanizing and liberating man that has inexhaustible potential. It is superior to any view of man that can offer no other purposes than self-assertion, a sense of accomplishment, the desire for admiration, and an increase of pleasure. When the Church critically reflects on her own history of following Christ, which is marked by both success and failings, she will take her bearings, not from models offered by materialistic anthropologies and immanentist explanations of the world, but rather from the essential features of her own view of man, which is rooted in divine revelation.

The Christian faith proceeds from the uncomplicated and felicitous insight that man cannot create himself and need not liberate himself on his own. With his creatureliness man also accepts himself in his sexually determined corporality, whereby he is ordered to the human community in the basic structures of individual and social life. The decisive factor in determining the relationship between the sexes is neither an abstract ideal of equality (transcending corporality) nor a dogmatic reduction of one sex to terms that more aptly describe the other. Christian theology is capable of seeing that the unity of mankind and its differentiation into the two sexes are equally primordial, a fact that it recognizes as a participation in God's goodness, which is communicated in the act of creation and which proves to be the ground of being for all creaturely existence and for the free exercise of responsibility. Being human—as a creature—means that man and woman, precisely in being different from one another, are equipped with independent personalities vis-à-vis their fellow men and also with respect to God. In their complementarity they are not restricted; rather it is being made *for* one another that makes them capable of realizing their personhood fully in relation *to* each other. Precisely in this interaction of being-in-relation and being-a-person, the image and likeness of God in man is manifested. Man is the image of God on the basis of the participation that is granted to him in God's *ipseity*, the positive character of his being himself [as well as being what-he-is], for God accomplishes his living, his knowing, and his loving in the interrelation of the three Divine Persons to each other as a *communio caritatis*.

Faith grasps as a positive datum the fact that man is created as male and female; this relieves man of the titanic and futile burden of trying to create himself in the first place and of having to fight for his or her dignity as a male or a female. Contrary to the oft-quoted remark of Simone de Beauvoir, man is in fact conceived and born as male or female. Society has to respect this, because man—as a male or as a female —is God's representative in the world and thus a creaturely personal mediator to immediacy with God. Man does not derive his value from some abstract ideal. He possesses and realizes concretely his personhood in his male or female corporality, at his biographical locale, in the historic succession of generations, and in his role within society long before anyone could attribute that personhood to him or render it controversial.

How—within the framework of the fundamental data of theological anthropology—has the mutuality of man and woman (parents, children, spouses, sibling) been experienced individually and concretized among the People of God of the Old and the New Covenant for the past 3500 years amid ever-varying societal conditions? This is a question that can only be comprehended and decided by means of the *theological* standards of Church historiography.

The schema that depicts history as an uninterrupted series of class conflicts between the oppressed and the oppressors, which is taken from Marxist thought and the ideology of emancipation, cannot be reconciled with the theological understanding of the origin, the mission, and the history of the Church. The relation between men and women in the Church, the Body of Christ, the People of God, and the Temple of the Holy Spirit, has nothing to do with the ideological view of history as a battle between the sexes for predominance and prestige.

Given a long history of millions upon millions of people of Jewish and Christian faith, you can produce as much evidence as you like of structural deficiencies and individual failures. All of this, however, cannot do away with the faith conviction and the fact, proved thousands of times, that the history of men and women (within the family and in marriage, at work, professionally and in public life, etc.) is not a history of oppression, exploitation, and degradation, but rather should be and is a history of love, for which God designed the physical and spiritual existence of man and of mankind.

It contradicts all responsible methods for arriving at historical judgments when one tries to evaluate the thought patterns and actions of men from epochs in the distant past according to contemporary standards and by comparison with today's priorities and possibilities in an industrialized information society that favors the presence of women in public life. Instead, one should strive to understand past customs from within the total context of an era and a cultural region—a context often containing many tensions and contradictions. The structural and individual conditions in which women lived in the Christian faith community and in markedly Christian societies (in Roman late antiquity and in the Middle Ages in the West until the seventeenth century) are perceived today as discriminatory, judging by our current ideals of equal rights in the working world and legal self-determination for women (and for men). Attempts to blame this on the allegedly authoritarian-patriarchal God of the Bible and on the man-centered view of humanity in

the Judaeo-Christian tradition prove, in the light of a theological and historico-critical assessment, to be ideological
constructs. Here history is not called on to help as a *magis-
tra vitae*, but rather is misused as an arsenal of weapons for
the ideological battle of the day. It is not a question then
of learning from history, but of morally discrediting one's
"opponent".

An ideology of history always needs a select group of institutions, events, and personages to charge with the sole
responsibility for all of "the world's misery", historical vil-
lains that provide an object for the indignation of those who
often fail to address the ethical challenges of their own time.
These rituals of indignation are provocations designed to si-
lence the "opponent". By having recourse largely to a pop-
ularized version of history, it seems very easy to trace all ag-
gressions, frustrations, and neuroses back to the (allegedly)
disturbed relations of the Church Fathers to sexuality and
to women.

In one department of feminist literature a blatant misin-
terpretation of biblical and doctrinal statements about God,
about creation, grace, sin, the Church, marriage, and sexuality, results from—among other determinants—the decision to interpret these things not so much with theological categories as with the Marxist historical thesis that all
ideas are merely the product of power struggles among social
classes and groups. Equally blind to the insights of a Christian anthropology grounded in faith in God is "Freudian"
psychoanalysis (in its vulgar form), which sees religion in
the first place and the doctrines and the practice of the faith
as things originating in wish fulfillment and sexual neuroses.
Beneath every magisterial teaching and behind every missionary and pastoral activity of the Church one can discern
only self-interested strategies for consolidating power or for

defending those who are in control from "anxieties" about the "people".

In the relevant literature one occasionally encounters the view that a male-dominated Church—harking back to the biblical prophecy about Eve's punishment, the Pauline prohibition of women teachers, the notion of a male, violent God, and the command that wives be submissive to their husbands—has declared women in the figure of Eve to be chiefly at fault for sin and mankind's misery; consequently that "the feminine principle" and sexuality have increasingly been demonized. Theologically, such a perspective is completely erroneous: original sin is not the consequence of sexual seduction but rather of Adam's and Eve's desire to "be like God". Such an interpretation of history is also contradicted by the simple fact that Mary, because of her faith, was very early on considered by Irenaeus of Lyons as the New Eve and the "cause of salvation . . . for the whole human race".[1] Historiographers would do well to note another circumstance: pagan contemporaries mocked the early Christians, because the women among them were on an equal footing with the men and made essential contributions to the demographics of the Church and to the way her spiritual mission was perceived.

It is completely unrealistic to think that from the very beginning of the human species males had organized as a conspiracy to dominate and oppress the female sex. The idea breaks down for the simple fact that all males are born of females, receive as children from their mothers everything that goes into being human, and even as adults are neither willing nor able to found a society without women. The Church has always been made up of men and women. The

---

[1] *Adversus haereses* 3, 22, 4; cf. also Augustine, *Sermo* 51, 2.

monk, too, and the priest living as a celibate each has a mother and sisters, has been acquainted with girls from his childhood and youth, knows from his struggle with his vocation what a woman means for a man—indeed, from the very decision to do without marriage and family—and in his catechetical and pastoral work has to deal with women, whom he should treat respectfully, like sisters or mothers (1 Tim 5:2). He is concerned about the success of marriages and of family life and accompanies the married faithful on their way with his care and assistance. In his spiritual life he takes his bearings from female saints as well: martyrs, foundresses, women doctors of the Church, and he recognizes the essential importance of women in salvation history, especially the role of Mary, the Mother of the Lord, whom he sees with "the eyes of faith" and who is anything but the product of an overheated religious imagination that wavers between divinizing and demonizing the feminine principle. Are those not, rather, the products of an imagination steeped in Gnosticism or theosophy—phantasms that have nothing to do with Christian faith and that are useless as explanations for the workings of the Divine Spirit? "Now we have received not the spirit of the world, but the Spirit which is from God, that we might understand the gifts bestowed on us by God. And we impart this in words not taught by human wisdom but taught by the Spirit, interpreting spiritual truths to those who possess the Spirit" (1 Cor 2:12–13).

Even though most Christian authors in antiquity and in the Middle Ages presuppose a certain preeminence of the male sex, there can be no question whatsoever of an ontological and essential gradation, as found in the Neoplatonic philosophies of emanation, and there is certainly no moral evaluation of the difference, as in Gnosticism. That would be diametrically opposed to Christian teaching about the goodness of creation, about personhood, and thus about personal mediation in divine immediacy, and such innovations have in fact been rejected as heretical.

From a theological perspective, the primary and ultimate criterion for the value and dignity of man is not to be found in the parameters of an ideology driven by achievement and consumption, but rather in relationship-as-a-person to God and to one's fellow men. This has its corollary in the doctrine that every baptized person is fully entitled as a child of God (Gal 3:28; Acts 2:17).

This is especially evident when it comes to describing man's place within the Church. Church is not a religious community consisting of a few people with an immediate mystical experience of unity with the divine abyss of Being and those consumers who get their religion second-hand. The Church of Jesus Christ is not a union with leaders and rank-and-file members, and certainly not a chain of command with officers and subordinates. Church is a community of human beings, called into life by God; these men and women, by virtue of their connection with Jesus Christ, personally make his salvific presence in the world visible and palpable, and they actualize the connections among themselves as the mutual service rendered by the members of the one Body of Christ. The decisive factor is the call to community with Jesus Christ in faith and in discipleship. Through Baptism believers are inserted into Christ's relationship to his Father as the Son of God (Gal 3:28; 4:4–6) through the power of the Spirit of Love deep in the heart of man (Rom 5:5).

Thus man and woman are capable of realizing their personhood in love for God and for one another in various states of life: marriage and "celibacy for the sake of the kingdom [of God]", which involves a special commitment to the

Church. The ideal is not an abstract, isolated equality before God. In personal relationship among human beings, who are differentiated as male and female, the human community, in Christ, presents a model for and a realization of fellowship with God. The essence of the Church cannot be stated any more succinctly. It may be that a largely secularized, post-Christian society will only be able to understand ministries in the Church (religion teacher, catechist, medical missionary, social worker) or honorary appointments (e.g., of women who serve as parish administrators, lectors, or extraordinary ministers of the Eucharist) or the service rendered by the bishop, priest, and deacon as a consequence of their ordination, through parallels drawn mostly from sociology. Nevertheless, within the Church it must be proclaimed in no uncertain terms that all ministries and missions originate in Christ's *diakonia* [service] and that all offices and services ultimately have reference to the *koinonia* [communion] created by the sacramental system.

Taking one's bearings from the Second Vatican Council's understanding of the Church makes it possible to see the essential ecclesiastical importance of the *mission* and of the *charism* of each individual Christian in collaboration with the ministry of the ordained priesthood. An image of the Church that is fixated on the priest betrays a "preconciliar" mind-set, but so does a job description for a lay apostolate performed at the expense of the sacramental ministry.

Only from the perspective of a consistently sacramental understanding of the Church will there be a correct and meaningful framing of the question, whether being male is intrinsically and irrevocably a prerequisite for receiving Holy Orders, or whether the Church's practice until now has been dependent upon de facto societal views as to what is plausible and possible.

Once a lay person is no longer incorrectly defined as a Christian who can do less and is less than a priest, and Holy Orders is no longer mistakenly understood as an intensification or even as the perfection of being a Christian, then the focus of the theme "equal rights and full participation of women in the Church" must also be widened beyond the narrow slogan of "women's ordination". That means that referring to the essential contribution of lay men and women toward the building up of the Church and the propagation of the Kingdom of God can no longer be dismissed as a diversionary tactic to steer them into subordinate forms of service. For the ministries and missions of the laity, too, give expression to the sacramental mission and structure of the Church, since they proceed from Baptism and Confirmation and participation in the Eucharist. In Mary, the Mother of the Lord, is prefigured the image of the Church as Bride and hearer of the Word, and the existential situation of the human being in the presence of God as a Spirit-filled believer (Lk 1:45; 11:27f.; Rev 22:17). If this is true, then there cannot be even the slightest doubt about the essential importance of the woman as an individual human being and of the feminine form in which humanity is realized. The vocation of the woman is portrayed in Scripture not only as that of a mother to her children (2 Tim 1:5) or of a wife to her husband who is not yet a believer (1 Pet 3:1), but also as a witness of our Lord's Resurrection to the entire Church in Mary Magdalen (Jn 20:17). "She is the Apostle of the apostles, so that, just as at first a woman exclaimed the words of death, now a woman transmits the words of life."[2]

The theme "women in the Church", which of course

---

[2] Thomas Aquinas, *Comm. in Joannem,* cap. 20, l. 3, 6.

the weighty problems of the Church in a secularized world cannot camouflage, could be a test case for a new capacity of Christians for dialogue with each other and for the Church's ability to hear and interpret the Word of God in Sacred Tradition and Sacred Scripture (DV 10).

The message that the Second Vatican Council addressed to women in 1965 remains relevant: "The hour is coming, the hour is already here in which the vocation of women is being realized fully, the hour in which woman is attaining an influence, an effectiveness, an unprecedented authority in society. That is why at this time, when humanity is experiencing such a profound transformation, women filled with the Spirit of the Gospel can do so much to keep humanity from declining."[3]

---

[3] AAS 58 (1966): 13f. [Translated from the original French.]

II

WHO RECEIVES THE SACRAMENT OF HOLY ORDERS IN THE DEGREES OF PRIESTHOOD AND DIACONATE?

1. The present status of the question about the possibility of women's ordination

In his apostolic letter *Ordinatio sacerdotalis* dated May 22, 1994, about "priestly ordination [which has] always been reserved to men alone", Pope John Paul II, invoking the fullness of his apostolic authority, reaffirmed the teaching that has been in effect since the beginning of the Church, "that the Church has no authority whatsoever to confer priestly ordination on women".[1] This "matter of great importance

---

[1] OS 4. On the dispute about theological competence and a possible revision of the teaching, see the article "Ordinatio sacerdotalis", by Gisbert Greshake, in LThK 7:1110f. (with bibliography). See also the careful judgment by Winfried Aymans, "Veritas de fide tenenda. Kanonistische Erwägungen zu dem Apostolischen Schreiben *Ordinatio sacerdotalis* im Lichte des Motu proprio *Ad tuendam fidem*", in Gerhard Ludwig Müller, ed., *Frauen in der Kirche: Eigensein und Mitverantwortung* (Würzburg, 1999), pp. 380–98 at pp. 397f. "In the case of the teaching in the apostolic letter *Ordinatio sacerdotalis* that priestly ordination is reserved to men alone, we are dealing with a *veritas de fide tenenda* [truth that is to be held *de fide*, as a matter of faith]. . . . Materially this teaching goes back to the Lord's selection and authorization of the Twelve, to which Sacred Scripture testifies. Throughout her history the Church has testified, by her actual practice, that she has understood the selection of men for the apostolic ministry, not as a circumstance dependent on the times, but rather as a deliberate course of action taken by the Lord. . . . The tradition of this understanding has been followed by the ordinary and universal Magis-

... pertains to the Church's divine constitution". Therefore this *praxis Ecclesiae* of conferring Holy Orders only on baptized males is a decree of *divine* law. This practice belongs to the "substance of the sacraments"[2] and hence definitively remains beyond the competence of the ecclesiastical authority, which governs within the framework of positive ecclesiastical law.

The apostolic letter qualified this unanimous practice and traditional teaching of the Church as being an expression of a doctrine contained in revelation (*tamquam divinitus revelatum*)[3] and distinguished it from usages that developed historically and from customs that, while sociologically determined, can in principle be changed. The immediate occasion for the document was the previous discussion in the Anglican communion about the possibility of ordaining women

---

terium, not particularly by means of doctrinal documents, however, but rather by the Church's practice. This does not signify, though, any intrinsic lack of tradition, since doctrinal statements are elicited chiefly to clarify existing differences in understanding and interpreting the faith. That is why constant practice, even when—or precisely when—it is not accompanied by corresponding doctrinal statements, is all the more of an expression of an undisputed understanding of practices that are rooted in revelation. Pope John Paul II, without making a formal definition yet calling attention to his authentic teaching authority, has verified and reaffirmed this appraisal of the Church's historical faith. The ultimate binding force in this aspect of the Church's understanding of the priestly office does not derive from papal affirmation, but rather from the tradition of the ordinary and universal Magisterium. It certainly could happen, though, that in some further development the extraordinary Magisterium of the Pope or of the college of bishops could be provoked to make a formal definition of this doctrine."

[2] Council of Trent, "Decree on Communion under Both Species" (1562), DH 1728; Pope Pius XII, apost. const. *Sacramentum ordinis* (1947), DH 3857.

[3] Vatican I, dogmatic constitution *Dei Filius*, chap. 3, DH 3011; Vatican II, LG 25.

as deacons and priests (presbyters and bishops), which in the United States of America, in other countries, and finally in the "Church of England", too, led to the ordination of women as deacons and priests. The Pope mentions in this connection the correspondence between Pope Paul VI and the primate of the Anglican ecclesial community, the archbishop of Canterbury, then the clarification of the Roman Curia's Congregation for the Doctrine of the Faith *Inter insigniores* (1976), as well as his own affirmation of the valid Church teaching in *Mulieris dignitatem*, dated August 15, 1988.

Within the Catholic Church the discussion about the dogmatic feasibility of sacramentally ordaining women to the ministries of deacon, priest, and bishop, that is, to the priestly ministry (which comprises three degrees of sacramental Orders and constitutes a hierarchy) first became a hotly debated topic in the parishes and among theologians after the Second Vatican Council.

2. Painful points in the present discussion

Doubts as to whether this practice reflects a truth contained in revelation are based essentially on two objections:

First, adopting the historically and systematically outmoded theses of the liberal theology of cultural [i.e., post-Enlightenment] Protestantism, many authors, even Catholics, dispute the immediate derivation of the priestly ministry from the apostolic ministry in the first-generation Church and therefore question the presence of the mission and the salvific ministry of the apostles in the ministry of the bishop, priest, and deacon.[4]

---

[4] "Frauen im Neuen Testament: Dienste und Ämter", in Müller, *Frauen*, pp. 231–51; citation at 231–33.

The false exegetical presuppositions that follow from a purely his-
toricist view of revelation and its development in the *sensus fidei* of
the Church have been analyzed and criticized by Karl Kertelge.

Already in 1994 Peter Hünermann, after the publication of *Ordinatio sacerdotalis*, had reported having "misgivings" with regard to it
(P. Hünermann, "*Schwerwiegende Bedenken: Eine Analyse des Apostolischen Schreibens* Ordinatio sacerdotalis", HK 48 [1994]: 406–
10), and in considering the biblical basis for the Pope's apostolic
letter, he had declared that the criterion of performing exegesis
according to the historico-critical method was of decisive importance. "The argumentation of this letter is conclusive given the
following presuppositions: (1) that the band of the Twelve, to
which men were called by Jesus Christ, is identical to the apostles and that the vocation of the Twelve and the vocation of the
apostles is one and the same; (2) that the apostles themselves formally and explicitly selected and installed successors in office,
bishops, who were men. Only under these two conditions is the
argumentation presented in *Ordinatio sacerdotalis* conclusive per
se" (ibid., p. 408).

Hünermann's criteriology proceeds from the correct assumption that the ministry of the apostles within the framework of the
"twelve apostles" and the handing on of this ministry to "successors in office" (*successio apostolica*) form the theological basis
for the priestly ministry of the Church (including the episcopal
ministry). What appears problematic in this, of course, is making the historico-critical distinction between the "Twelve" called
by Jesus and the post-Resurrectional "Apostles", as well as the
"formal and explicit" installation of successors in office by the
"twelve apostles" the criterion for the truth of this starting point.

Hünermann, citing the "majority of more significant Catholic
and Lutheran New Testament scholars" (which three lines later
suddenly becomes the "consensus of Catholic exegetes"), calls
into question the existence of historical evidence for the two
conditions that he has set up, and thus the judgment on *Ordinatio
sacerdotalis* is pronounced (ibid., p. 409). What papal document,
or what encyclical, indeed which decree or which constitution
of Vatican II can still be adhered to in those parts referring to the
Bible, according to such an absolutist application of the criteria

of the historico-critical method? . . . This blatant unfairness of a judgment that needs simply to be stated [to be "conclusive"] calls our attention to the fact that the historico-critical exegesis cannot be the sole criterion for Catholic theology. . . .

In the document of the Pontifical Biblical Commission, too, *The Interpretation of the Bible in the Church* (April 23, 1993), it is conceded that the historico-critical method has, among the various methods, a particular preeminence and reliably "opens up to the modern reader a path to the meaning of the biblical text" (Pontifical Biblical Commission, *The Interpretation of the Bible in the Church* [April 23, 1993], St. Paul Books and Media, Boston, p. 42). But it does not replace the hermeneutic of "the interpretation of the Bible in the Church". Finally, if it is to be methodical, the work of the Catholic exegete, according to this document, must have some connection with the "living tradition of the Church, whose first concern is fidelity to the revelation attested by the Bible" (ibid., p. 88).

If the authority to preach and pastoral ministry were no more than the actualization of the mission entrusted to the Church as a whole, then it would in fact be the Church's prerogative to appoint individual members of the community to the specific exercise of the universal ministry. The difference between laity and priests, which has a sacramental basis, would then dwindle into a functional difference between honorary officials and chief officials who professionally proclaimed the Word, administered the sacraments, and organized the externals of community life. With that, though, one of the pervasive characteristics of Catholic (and Orthodox) ecclesiology—the qualitative difference between the common participation of all baptized persons in the prophetic and priestly mission of Jesus Christ by reason of their Baptism and the authorization of individual Christians in the Sacrament of Holy Orders—would be called into question and the Catholic understanding of the Church would be unhinged/turned upside down. The authority to make Christ, as Head of the Church, effectively present in the midst of the community of believers, though, is conferred through a special sacrament, in order to make it clear through outward signs that Christ is always the origin and source of all ecclesiastical life.

> Though they differ essentially and not only in degree, the common priesthood of the faithful and the ministerial or hierarchical priesthood are none the less ordered one to another; each in its own proper way shares in the one priesthood of Christ. The ministerial priest, by the sacred power that he has, forms and rules the priestly people; in the person of Christ he effects the eucharistic sacrifice and offers it to God in the name of all the people. The faithful indeed, by virtue of their royal priesthood, participate in the offering of the Eucharist. They exercise that priesthood, too, by the reception of the sacraments, prayer and thanksgiving, the witness of a holy life, abnegation and active charity. (LG 10)

The Church can never declare herself autonomous over and against Christ, whose Body and social expression she is. The Church is not only the creation of the Word, which continually proceeds anew from the proclamation of the gospel. Above and beyond that, she is the creation of the Word-made-flesh, of the Son of God forever living in the Church as *Christus praesens*. He gave his apostles a share in his mission, so that "[i]n the person of the bishops . . . , to whom the priests render assistance, the Lord Jesus Christ, supreme high priest, is present in the midst of the faithful."[5] The Jesus who proclaims and heals can never be reduced to the Christ who is proclaimed. He remains always, precisely in his action within the Church and through her upon humanity as well, the *subject* of redemption and the communication of divine grace.

[5] LG 21.

Second, the traditional practice and doctrine is being confronted with the suspicion or the accusation of discrimination against women. In reality, any treatment of the female sex as inferior contradicts not only the recognition of human rights in modern constitutional states, but also and much more fundamentally those articles of the Catholic faith concerning the full personal dignity of every human being and the vocation of women and men to believe, to become full members of the Church, and to enter into communion with the triune God. The ultimate perfection of every created person is nothing less than the love that God *is* in himself and that he sent to us in the Incarnation of his Word and the outpouring of his Spirit. The questions to be discussed are, whether the Church's practice of ordaining only men as bishops, priests, and deacons objectively constitutes a form of discrimination against women, and whether this practice depended only on purely historical circumstances, e.g., erroneous sociological and psychological notions about the mutuality and complementarity of men and women in social life—notions which also had had an effect upon the self-understanding of the ecclesial community and which should be changed today.

Within the context of these questions, important problems of theological epistemology, of ecclesiology, and of theological anthropology are addressed. In the debate about these themes, especially when it is reported in the mass media, clichés with little basis in fact and stereotyped notions about historical and cultural connections often make themselves heard, and these lead to judgments that are not relevant.

Any search for an appropriate answer to this new and volatile question must take its measure using the tools and methodologies of Catholic theology and must take its bearings, as to its content, from the sources of revelation and of the Church's tradition of faith. A "hermeneutic of suspicion"—which presumes that it is just a matter of self-interest and maintaining power on the part of those who already possess the priesthood as a privilege of their class—is a bad counselor, because such an interpretation of the biblical, historical, and magisterial data is founded upon a questionable presupposition about Church and priesthood, about faith and theology. One problem with this hermeneutic—and by no means the last one—is that it ignores the anthropological dogma of the equal personal dignity of man and woman.

Defining man in his relationship to God leads to a much more radical expression of the dignity of woman, as a person and in her full participation in the life of Christ's Church, than any social ideology could ever provide, since that can have reference only to changes in legal status and social structures.

3. A change of strategy: If not the priesthood, then at least the diaconate

"What do you think about women's ordination?" is the crucial question posed incessantly in the churches of the "first world". Everyone gets tested on whether his views are progressive or conservative. The vote in favor of a women's diaconate, which the bishops are then supposed to communicate to Rome, has become part of the ritual at synods, academic conferences, and workshops [in German-speaking lands]. Whether we are dealing here with an expression of the *sensus fidei*, the Church's faith-consciousness, is of course not something that can be decided on the basis of majority opinion. The criterion must be, rather, to what extent does the petition agree with scriptural teaching, apostolic tradition, and the doctrinal pronouncements of the Church.

One sector within the feminist movement meanwhile, in response to the Pope's doctrinal decision in *Ordinatio sacerdotalis* (1994), has set aside the question of priestly ordination for women and now concentrates on the sacramental ordination of women to the diaconate. The most recent magisterial documents present the impossibility of ordaining women to the priesthood as a dogma, that is, as something pertaining to the Church's deposit of faith; yet ordination to the diaconate is not mentioned explicitly; therefore some believe that this question remains open and can be examined separately.

*A response to Dorothea Reininger's
study on the diaconate of women*[6]

On the basis of this problematic interpretation of *Ordinatio sacerdotalis*, Ms. Reininger devotes her voluminous dissertation to the question of whether women can *validly* and *licitly* receive sacramental ordination to the diaconate (p. 27). Canon 1024 of the 1983 *Code of Canon Law* (CIC/1983) and the corresponding canon from the *Canons of the Oriental Churches* (CCEO can. 754, §1) state that only a baptized man can validly receive Holy Orders; since they are only laws of the Church and not divine law, the argument goes, the pope can make an exception in the case of diaconal ordination.

The central thesis of the book is formulated as follows: "A reintroduction of the women's diaconate . . . would in

[6] Dorothea Reininger, *Diakonat der Frau in der einen Kirche* (Ostfildern, 1999).

this context be understood as a logical step away from perceived discrimination toward a real recognition of the equal
dignity of man and woman. In the diaconate the Church
could gain a structure that would effectively model the partnership of man and woman, of deacon and deaconess—as
recommended by the German bishops" (p. 132).

Was the office of the deaconess part of Holy Orders?

A consecration of deaconesses has been noted since the time
of the *Apostolic Constitutions* (a collection, compiled around
380, of older ecclesiastical ordinances). The author [i.e., Ms.
Reininger] rightly recognizes that the decisive question is the
dogmatic one about its sacramental quality (p. 117). With
this in mind she turns, in part 1 of her study, to a "discussion
of the women's diaconate in the Roman Catholic Church"
(pp. 41-171).

The author's efforts to maintain theological objectivity
are salutary and welcome. The argument dispenses with
most, if not all, of the usual clichés about the misogynistic
Church Fathers. The search for motives rooted in a fear of
women and the sexual neuroses of those who want to "hold
women off" at the entrance to the walled city of ordained
ministry is relegated to the footnotes as an unwarranted bit
of pastoral psychology.

The conclusive evidence must consist of the dogmatic
statements found in relevant sources. These, of course, cannot simply be cited without further comment. The author
starts with the New Testament beginnings of the Church
and proceeds beyond the development of the ministry of
deaconesses in the third and fourth centuries up to the early
Middle Ages, when this ministry was de facto extinct in both
the West and the East. The trouble is that the terms *diakonos*,

diakonein, and *diakonia* were applied to very different sorts of functions and activities. Both the servants at the wedding feast in Cana and Christ himself, the apostles as well as their coworkers and the Christians who performed any sort of ancillary services whatsoever in the community: all were called "servants" (= *diakonos*) on account of their service, without this being understood, of course, as the designation for an office or ministry within the one Sacrament of Holy Orders. Here the author could have made it clearer that the development of a specific official title occurs in passages where deacons are mentioned together with bishops (for the first time in Phil 1:1), and not at Romans 16:1, where Phoebe is styled a woman-servant. For contemporary linguistic usage it is crucial to distinguish among the three ministerial degrees of the one sacramental *Ordo*, and to designate other responsibilities entrusted to the laity as "ecclesiastical offices" (LG 33). The author misleads her readers with the somewhat unspecified terminology of "the" offices in the Church. When in his work entitled *To the Christian Nobility* (1520)[7] Luther rejected the terms "priesthood" and "sacrament" and introduced instead for all ecclesiastical functions the term "offices" [*Ämter*], which he adopted from the secular realm, the fundamental meaning of apostolic ministry was at stake. The reformer's views notwithstanding, it must

[7] "An Appeal to the Ruling Class of German Nationality as to the Amelioration of the State of Christendom", in: John Dillenberger, ed., *Martin Luther: Selections from His Writings* (Garden City, N.Y.: Anchor Books, 1961), pp. 403–85. "When a bishop consecrates, he simply acts on behalf of the entire congregation, all of whom have the same authority. They may select one of their number and command him to exercise this authority on behalf of the others. . . . It follows that the status of a priest among Christians is merely that of an office-bearer; while he holds the office he exercises it; if he be deposed he resumes his status in the community and becomes like the rest [*literally*: he is a farmer or a townsman like everyone else]" (pp. 408–9).

be grasped that the relation to the ministry of the bishop and the priest is the genuine criterion for determining whether one can speak of a specific participation in the "apostolic ministry" or of an "ecclesiastical office" in the more general sense (1 Tim 3; *Didache* 15; 1 Clement 42–44).

This is how the Second Vatican Council presents the Catholic understanding of ministry, as it describes the services of the successor to the apostles (= bishop), which by virtue of a divine arrangement proceed from the apostolic mission and are ordered to the unity of the local church, and the subordinate sacerdotal service of the presbyters and the diaconal service of still other persons:

> That divine mission, which was committed by Christ to the apostles, is destined to last until the end of the world (cf. Mt 28:20). . . . For that very reason the apostles were careful to appoint successors in this hierarchically constituted society. . . . They accordingly designated such men and then made the ruling that likewise on their death other proven men should take over their ministry. . . . In that way, then, with priests and deacons as helpers, the bishops received the charge of the community. (LG 20)

Here the bishops and presbyters represent the *sacerdotium*, to which the degree within the Sacrament of Holy Orders called the "diaconate" is subordinate, as a ministry assisting that of the bishop and the presbyter. The bishops and presbyters act in the Person of Christ as Head of the Church, whereas the deacons stand by the bishops and presbyters and act with them in their functions *directed toward the Church*, while the lower clerics, from the subdeacon downward, are *drawn from the community* and are ordered to the priesthood and the diaconate. The Council of Trent, too, understands Holy Orders in this way (DH 1763f.; 1772): The sacrament is constituted on the foundation of the priesthood of bishop and presbyter, and to it are ordered the higher and lower degrees of the clergy; of the higher degrees only the diaconate dates back to apostolic times. The doctrine of the two holy orders, namely, the *sacerdotium* and the diaconate, is clearly discernible in Hippolytus' writings (*Apostolic Tradition* 3–8), which represent the Roman and Alexandrine tradition. This doctrine became influential also in the medieval Scholastic teaching on the sacramental *Ordo*.[8]

Theologically this distinction of *sacerdotium* and diaconate within the one Sacrament of Holy Orders, as handed down by the Church's Magisterium, is interpreted as follows, e.g., by Thomas Aquinas (*Summa theologiae, Suppl.* 37, 4 *ad* 3):

> The offerings made by the people are offered through the priest. Hence a two-fold ministry is necessary with regard to offerings. One on the part of the people; and this belongs to the subdeacon, who receives the offerings from the people and places them on the altar or offers them to the deacon; the other is on the part of the priest, and belongs to the deacon, who hands the offerings to the priest. This is the principal act of both Orders, and for this reason the deacon's Order is higher.

The subdiaconate is an *ordo maior non sacramentalis* (in contradistinction to the degrees of the *sacerdotium* and the diaconate instituted by the apostles, which the apostles instituted by a divine decree [*Suppl.* 37, 1 *ad* 2], the lower clerical degrees originated in the Church's customary law). This passage from Thomas also makes clear that not every consecration and blessing is a sacrament (*Suppl.* 34, 3 *ad* 3) or belongs to Holy Orders as a degree. The criterion for belonging to the sacramental higher orders is whether or not the degree is ordered to the full priestly authority. For this purpose only the priest and the deacon receive the imposition of hands, but with this distinction: Only the *sacerdos* acts *in persona Christi capitis* (*Suppl.* 37, 4 *ad* 2), while the deacon shares in the priestly action *per participationem*. Although the latter cannot effect the Consecration as the priest does, he assists the priest by carrying out the priestly activity of distributing Holy Communion (*Summa contra gentiles* 4, 75).

---

[8] Cf. Isidore of Seville, *Etym.* 7, 12; Peter Lombard, *Sent.* 4, 24, 10; *Decretum Gratiani*: Friedberg 1:750; Synod of Benevento, 1098, can. 1, DH 703; Pope Innocent III, DH 785; Pope Gregory IX, DH 826; cf. also DH 1315, 1326, 1630, 1697, 1719, and 3317.

The consecration of deaconesses was not an ordination of women to the diaconate

The institutionalization of charitable services performed by widows in the Christian community, of the assistance rendered by women during baptismal ceremonies, and of liturgical functions in a convent of consecrated virgins is apparent from the beginning of the third century in the ecclesiastical neologism: *diaconissa/diacona*. For Koiné Greek, unlike Latin, could not construct the female form of "servant" by a change of ending, but could only indicate it with the feminine article (cf. Rom 16:1). Aside from that, we also encounter the title *diaconissa* (and, similarly, *presbyterissa* and *episcopissa*) as a designation for the wives of deacons— for example, in papal instructions or conciliar canons that admonish higher clerics to practice celibacy, in the sense of continence.

Although there are records of the liturgical installation of deaconesses dating back to the fourth century, one must not overlook the fact that the selfsame authors who testify to this practice also make clear that the consecration of deaconesses was not the ordination of women to the diaconal ministry; on the contrary, it was a question of a different ecclesiastical office.[9] To the early Church it was clear that, without prejudice to the various degrees of bishop, presbyter, and deacon, which assumed a definitive form in the transition to the postapostolic age, these ministries owe their existence to the historical initiative of the apostles and to the special presence of the Holy Spirit in the foundational phase of the Church; whereas the later, so-called nonsacramental

---

[9] Supporting references can be found in: Gerhard Ludwig Müller, ed., *Der Empfänger des Weihesakraments: Quellen zur Lehre und Praxis der Kirche, nur Männern das Weihesakrament zu spenden* (Würzburg, 1999).

consecrations were introduced by ecclesiastical authorities
and thus are not matters of divine law but only of Church
law. An undifferentiated way of speaking about the variety
of official structures in the New Testament—from which
the model of the threefold ministry supposedly was then selected arbitrarily sometime during the course of the second
century—is at the basis of Ms. Reininger's study, too.

A sacramental understanding of the office is
incompatible with the functional specifications

Of course Jesus did not "found" a church, in the technical sense understood by corporate law, and arbitrarily determine its ministerial structure. His eschatological work of
instituting the Kingdom of God, rather, is centered on his
mission from the Father, in which he has included the apostles. The individual strands of New Testament writings do
not exhibit various forms of sociological organization, but
rather testify that the handing on of the apostolic mission
took shape under the influence of the glorified Lord, whose
Spirit was at work within his Church, which is his Body
and thus the visible form of his presence in the world. This
constitutes a sacramental view of the Church and thus of
the kerygmatic and pastoral ministry as well—a view that
is diametrically opposed to a "corporate law" view of the
Church and a functionalist understanding of ministry. It is
a doctrine binding in faith that in the Sacrament of Holy
Orders the mission and authority of the apostles are passed
on in varying degrees for the building up of the Church
through the proclamation of the gospel, the administration
of the sacramental signs, and the pastoral ministry. Without
prejudice to the uniform terminology that was established
only at the end of the first century, there is in every local

church, by dint of apostolic initiatives and by virtue of a divine arrangement, a bishop, who represents the unity of the church with its apostolic origin and the *communio* that it enjoys with the other local churches that are in union with the Catholic Church; there is also the college of presbyters, which is subordinate to him, and there are the deacons, who are placed at "the service of the bishop" (*ministerium episcopi*). From the time of Hippolytus of Rome (early third century), the closely associated service of the bishop and the presbyters was termed the *sacerdotium*, as distinguished from the *ministerium* of the deacons. The *sacerdotium* is the nucleus of the apostolic, spiritual authority of the bishops and priests, which continues to exist in the Sacrament of Holy Orders. To them is ordered, within the Sacrament of Orders, the degree of the diaconate, so that all of the general, essential characteristics of Holy Orders apply to the diaconate as well. Pius XII already, in the apostolic constitution *Sacramentum ordinis* (1947), emphasized the unity of the three degrees of Holy Orders, as understood by tradition in its entirety; then Vatican II in *Lumen gentium* pellucidly set forth the certain doctrine about the unity of Holy Orders, which (though often overlooked) is in complete continuity with the teaching of the Council of Trent. Given these two magisterial precedents, there can be no reasonable doubt that the degree of the sacramentally ordained deacon is also intended in *Ordinatio sacerdotalis*. Splitting the one *Ordo* into three more or less free-standing sacraments, which is the basis of the recent strategy, supposedly in keeping with *Ordinatio sacerdotalis*, is totally indefensible theologically. Therefore it is quite regrettable that the absolutely crucial and fundamental project of surveying the biblical, historico-dogmatic, and magisterial evidence was not carried out thoroughly, but was only "sketched" (p. 56). A survey based on the secondary literature, which the author has certainly examined to a remarkable extent, is not a sufficient basis for an objective judgment. Where there is doubt, the majority of scholars then tip the scale. The supreme authority, over and over again, is Peter Hünermann. His opponent, who is always effortlessly refuted, is Manfred Hauke.[10] Hünermann almost rates as a *Church Father* and as the ultimate academic authority, superior to the Church's *Magisterium*, even though his works on precisely these topics raise considerable doubts about the historical and systematic reliability of his arguments.

How misleading it can be to rely on quotations from the secondary literature when researching the history of dogma is evident, e.g., in the passage that repeats the thesis introduced in the seventeenth century by the Reformed theologian Jacques Basnage, that the Council of Nicaea in canon 18 forbade deacons to celebrate the Eucharist, as though they had previously had the authority to effect the Consecration (cf. p. 618). In reality the Council forbids deacons to take it upon themselves to *administer* Communion to the presbyters and bishops (COD 14f.). For Basnage, naturally, there was no difference between the distribution of the Lord's Supper and the authority to consecrate, which is unknown to him as a Reformed theologian.

Similarly, a passage from St. Ambrose, *De officiis ministrorum* 1, 41, 205 (PL 16, 84), was often misinterpreted on the Protestant side for controversial purposes. In it the deacon St. Lawrence asks the bishop for permission to suffer martyrdom with him, since the latter as a priest never offered the Holy Sacrifice without his deacon. Since the bishop also entrusted to him the consecrated Blood of the Lord for

---

[10] Manfred Hauke, *Die Problematik um das Frauenpriestertum vor dem Hintergrund der Schöpfungs- und Erlösungsordnung* (Paderborn, 1982, and subsequent editions); English trans.: *Women in the Priesthood? A Systematic Analysis in the Light of the Order of Creation and Redemption*, trans. David Kipp (San Francisco: Ignatius Press, 1988).

distribution, he should be willing now to pour out together with
him his own blood in martyrdom. Ambrose presupposes the different
functions of priest and deacon at the celebration of the Eucharist,
which Justin Martyr had already demonstrated in 1 *Apol.* 65. The
presbyter pronounces the words of Consecration, while the deacon
assists him in distributing Holy Communion (cf. the extensive discussion in J. Forget's article "*Diacres*", DThC 4 [1939]: 703–31 at
714).

In her conclusion, Ms. Reininger states that admitting women to diaconal ordination is not compulsory according to
Scripture, tradition, and Church teaching, but that neither is
it necessarily ruled out. In her view, anyone who rejects in
principle the (re-)introduction of the female diaconate, citing dogmatic reasons or even the *ius divinum* [divine law] (p.
126), is guilty of an innovation that deviates from the faith.

Can dogmatic problems be decided by pastoral considerations?

Since the question has reached a dogmatic stalemate, as it
were, pastoral reasons for such a reintroduction could be
the decisive ones, according to our author's opinion. An *ar-
gumentum ad hominem* common in the early Church, namely,
that the ordination of women was not fitting and that it
would cause the pagans to ridicule the Church, is piquantly
twisted around so as to imply that the introduction of ordained ministry for women is positively necessary today if
the Church is to appear credible in the eyes of the neo-
pagans. Many of our contemporaries, she says, shake their
heads when they see the Church campaigning in the secular
realm for equal rights for women and men, while paradox-
ically not admitting women within her own ranks to positions of leadership or sharing power with them (cf. p. 120).
A peculiar argument, to make the pagans' and neo-pagans'
lack of understanding for Church teachings and the fear of

their laughter into a criterion for the Church's policy and doctrine!

In order to tip the scales in favor of introducing a sacramental ordination of women to the diaconate (N.B., not for the reinstatement of the early Church institution of deaconesses, who certainly were *not* women who had received a sacrament ordaining them to the diaconate), the author describes, one after the other in the wide-ranging second part of her study (pp. 173–602), the theological considerations, the decisions, and the pastoral experiences of the non-Catholic churches in which there is a women's diaconate comparable to the Catholic diaconal ministry: the churches of the Reformation, especially the Anglican Church—in which case the comparison is made difficult, of course, by the fundamental problem of whether ministry is understood in functional or sacramental terms; then the so-called Old Catholic Church; and finally the Orthodox Churches, which are in fact quite relevant to Catholic dogmatic teaching on this question; and finally there is a look at the treatment of this theme in the more recent documents from the ecumenical dialogue.

Contrary to our author's opinion, which is based on the assumption that the office of deaconess in the early Church was identical to the sacramental diaconal ministry, to which women today ought to be admitted "again", it should be clearly understood that we are dealing here with two different things. There can be no question of a "re"-introduction of a ministry for deaconesses that was "originally" sacramental but was forgotten in the course of time. An attempt to draw a parallel with the reintroduction of the diaconate as a permanent ministry, which was undertaken at the recommendation of Vatican II, is simply misleading. For the sacramental character of the diaconate was always maintained by the Magisterium. The difference between the permanent

diaconate and the diaconate as a preparation for the priesthood has its basis, not in sacramental theology, but in canon
law and is thus a matter of ecclesiastical discipline.

The job description for the female diaconate has no theological foundation

In part 3 (pp. 604–74), the dogmatic arguments in part 1
and the pastoral and ecumenical considerations in part 2
are utilized to delineate perspectives and develop visions for
a sacramental diaconate for women. In conclusion the author makes a plea for the necessity and appropriateness of
introducing a women's diaconate. On the authority of Peter
Hünermann (the same scholar who shattered all theological
and magisterial arguments by declaring them incomprehensible to him), we learn that the International Theological
Congress held in Stuttgart in 1997 finally and definitively
determined that an appeal to further theological clarification
would no longer be in keeping with "the present state of
research" (p. 679). Anyone who takes the signs of the times
seriously knows that it is not dogmatic arguments that stand
in the way of introducing a women's diaconate; rather, that
there are plenty of equal-opportunity reasons, which must
compel the Church to take action eventually. When you describe the problem that way, it is not surprising that Christian politicians are advocating public funding of educational
programs for future deaconesses; after all, they wish the
Church well and only mean to help out the authorities in
"Rome" and to "make some progress at last".

In the final analysis, though, the dogmatic justification for
all these pastoral considerations and for these attempts to for-
mulate a concrete job description remains undetermined, as
the bishop of Mainz hints with polite restraint in his fore-

word (p. 23): How are we to understand the consecration of deaconesses that was legitimately carried out in the Catholic Church, and what relation does that have to the diaconal ministry, which represents one degree in the threefold Sacrament of Holy Orders in the Catholic Church? The interpretations of Thiermeyer, Vagaggini, Evangelos Theodorou, et al., which are summarized very well (pp. 94–113; 503–37), are interesting. The question remains, however: How has the Church's Magisterium, which is authorized (not exclusively but ultimately and in a binding way) to articulate the Church's faith, judged the consecration of deaconesses, and also of subdeacons and abbesses, as well as other consecrations and blessings of persons, vis-à-vis the Sacrament of Holy Orders? It is true that one cannot simply apply the now normative concept of sacrament that was developed with precision in the twelfth century to documents from the fourth and fifth centuries, at least not without making careful hermeneutic transitions. Still, the question must be raised as to whether the essential elements of this concept of sacrament were [already] contained, by the very nature of the subject, in the holy signs of the Church that back then were termed the "real and true sacrament" as distinguished from the sacramentals. It was a fundamental belief of the Church, from the patristic age until the elaboration of sacramental theology in the Middle Ages, that only ordination to the *sacerdotium* (bishop and presbyter) and to the *ministerium* of the deacons, who were ordered immediately to the priest's service at the altar, could be considered as the sacrament instituted by the historical and glorified Christ, since only these three degrees of Holy Orders (regardless of how they developed and became differentiated from one another) date back to the apostolic beginnings of the Church. Contrary to the opinion expressed in the book at issue, the standard theological authors, the councils, and the papal decisions with respect to sacramental doctrine were thoroughly cognizant of the early Church institution of deaconesses, and by no means did they reject it for hostile, misogynistic reasons. In his commentary on 1 Timothy 3:11, for instance, Thomas Aquinas says with many other authors, citing Chrysostom, that since apostolic times there have been only three degrees of Holy Orders in the Church (prescinding from the subdiaconate, which was of importance in later canon law because of the obligation to practice celibacy, but which was not numbered among the sacramental *sacri ordines*). The Apostle [Paul], he continues, really does speak here of deaconesses, because women held an office of service in the community. This, however, is not to be confused with the diaconal ministry, because in the Greek of that time *diakonein* could be used for any and every form of service, which is particularly true of the Christian widows mentioned in 1 Timothy 5 [:3–16].

In "*De diaconissarum ordinatione*" (*Acta Sanctorum*, September 1, Antwerp 1746, I–XXVIII), a comprehensive study that takes into consideration all the patristic and Scholastic texts, Johannes Pinius states by way of introduction:

> Before I begin my presentation on the consecration of deaconesses, I wish to alert the reader that we are not dealing here with a consecration in the strict or sacramental sense of the word [i.e., "ordination"]. Rather it is a matter of a ceremonial consecration, that is, a consecration in the figurative sense, as I will demonstrate later in detail. We know of a practice of consecrating deaconesses, though, from the Fathers, the councils, from imperial edicts, and also from the liturgical books of the Eastern Churches.

With that he merely sets forth what Hippolytus already says in the *Apostolic Tradition* (*Traditio apostolica* 10). That the imposition of hands that later became customary in the consecration of deaconesses was understood, not sacramentally, but only as a blessing is shown very clearly in the *Apostolic Constitutions* 8, 28: "The deacon does not consecrate and does not give the blessing, but he receives it from the bishop and presbyter. He does not baptize and does not offer the sacrifice, but he takes from the sacrifice of the bishop or presbyter and communicates it to the people, not as a presbyter, but in the service of the presbyters. None of the remaining clerics [i.e., the lower clerics] is permitted to exercise the deacon's ministry." It follows from this that: "The deaconess does not bless and performs none of those duties whatsoever that the priests and deacons perform" (ibid.). We find the same thing in the Order of Imposition of Hands among the Syrian Nestorians: "The bishop places his hand on the head of the deaconess, not by way of imposing hands, but rather blessing her with a benediction . . ." (G. L. Müller, *Quellen* [see footnote 9 above], p. 262).

This view has been adopted by the Magisterium in all the great pronouncements on Holy Orders as a divinely revealed truth about the essence of the Sacrament of Orders. There is not one single pronouncement of the Magisterium that would call into question the connection between the sacramental diaconal ministry (insofar as it is understood as a distinct degree rooted in the *one* Sacrament of Orders and not as a particular ecclesiastical office of service) and baptized males. In view of the unanimity of tradition, attempts to dispute the sacramental character of the diaconate must also be rejected as clearly heretical.

While acknowledging the indisputable services rendered by the book at issue and the wealth of ecumenical information that it contains, there remains a striking disproportion between the theological part and the ecumenical and pastoral discussions. The sections treating the history of doctrine and systematic theology have turned out to be decidedly too short. For this reason, unfortunately, it must be said: the author still owes the discussion among scholars and the competent ecclesiastical authorities whom she addresses a demonstration of the dogmatic justification for her program of a "revival of the early Church's office of deaconess and a contemporary adaptation of it to the pastoral conditions and needs of the third millennium which is beginning" (p. 680). It is not, after all, a matter of modifying the office of deaconess found in the early Church so as to arrive at some form of ecclesiastical office with a brand-new set of functions; rather it is a question of whether or not the consecration of deaconesses was an independent sacramental degree within the one Sacrament of Holy Orders and whether it was also received by the Church as binding in faith.

4. Notes on a hermeneutic for magisterial documents and on the interpretation of theological sources

What kind of an answer do the biblical and historical dogmatic sources produce? Vatican II, in the Dogmatic Constitution on Divine Revelation, *Dei Verbum* (articles 7–10) summarized the theological hermeneutic for arriving at the definitive interpretation of Scripture and of other documents that make up the Church's tradition.

> 7. God graciously arranged that the things he had once revealed for the salvation of all peoples should remain in their entirety, throughout the ages, and be transmitted to all generations. Therefore, Christ the Lord, in whom the entire Revelation of the most high God is summed up (cf. 2 Cor 1:20; 3:16—4:6) commanded the apostles to preach the Gospel, which had been promised beforehand by the prophets, and which he fulfilled in his own person and promulgated with his own lips. In preaching the Gospel they were to communicate the gifts of God to all men. This Gospel was to be the source of all saving truth and moral discipline. This was faithfully done: it was done by the apostles who handed on, by the spoken

word of their preaching, by the example they gave, by the institutions they established, what they themselves had received —whether from the lips of Christ, from his way of life and his works, or whether they had learned it at the prompting of the Holy Spirit; it was done by those apostles and other men associated with the apostles who, under the inspiration of the same Holy Spirit, committed the message of salvation to writing.

In order that the full and living Gospel might always be preserved in the Church the apostles left bishops as their successors. They gave them "their own position of teaching authority." This sacred Tradition, then, and the sacred Scripture of both Testaments, are like a mirror, in which the Church, during its pilgrim journey here on earth, contemplates God, from whom she receives everything, until such time as she is brought to see him face to face as he really is (cf. 1 Jn 3:2).

8. Thus, the apostolic preaching, which is expressed in a special way in the inspired books, was to be preserved in a continuous line of succession until the end of time. Hence the apostles, in handing on what they themselves had received, warn the faithful to maintain the traditions which they had learned either by word of mouth or by letter (cf. 2 Thess 2:15); and they warn them to fight hard for the faith that had been handed on to them once and for all (cf. Jude 3). What was handed on by the apostles comprises everything that serves to make the People of God live their lives in holiness and increase their faith. In this way the Church, in her doctrine, life and worship, perpetuates and transmits to every generation all that she herself is, all that she believes.

The Tradition that comes from the apostles makes progress in the Church, with the help of the Holy Spirit. There is a growth in insight into the realities and words that are being passed on. This comes about in various ways. It comes through the contemplation and study of believers who ponder these things in their hearts (cf. Lk 2:19 and 51). It comes from the intimate sense of spiritual realities which they experience. And it comes from the preaching of those who have received, along with their right of succession in the episcopate, the sure charism of truth. Thus, as the centuries go by, the Church is always advancing towards the plenitude of divine truth, until eventually the words of God are fulfilled in her.

The sayings of the Holy Fathers are a witness to the life-giving presence of this Tradition, showing how its riches are poured out in the practice and life of the Church, in her belief and her prayer. By means of the same Tradition the full canon of the sacred books is known to the Church and the holy Scriptures themselves are more thoroughly understood and constantly actualized in the Church. Thus God, who spoke in the past, continues to converse with the spouse of his beloved Son. And the Holy Spirit, through whom the living voice of the Gospel rings out in the Church—and through her in the world—leads believers to the full truth, and makes the Word of Christ dwell in them in all its richness (cf. Col 3:16).

9. Sacred Tradition and sacred Scripture, then, are bound closely together, and communicate one with the other. For both of them, flowing out from the same divine well-spring, come together in some fashion to form one thing, and move towards the same goal. Sacred Scripture is the speech of God as it is put down in writing under the breath of the Holy Spirit. And Tradition transmits in its entirety the Word of God which has been entrusted to the apostles by Christ the Lord and the Holy Spirit. It transmits it to the successors of the apostles so that, enlightened by the Spirit of truth, they may faithfully preserve, expound and spread it abroad by their preaching. Thus it comes about that the Church does not draw her certainty about all revealed truths from the holy Scriptures alone. Hence, both Scripture and Tradition must be accepted and honored with equal feelings of devotion and reverence.

10. Sacred Tradition and sacred Scripture make up a single

sacred deposit of the Word of God, which is entrusted to the Church. By adhering to it the entire holy people, united to its pastors, remains always faithful to the teaching of the apostles, to the brotherhood, to the breaking of the bread and the prayers (cf. Acts 2:42 Greek). So, in maintaining, practicing and professing the faith that has been handed on there should be a remarkable harmony between the bishops and the faithful.

But the task of giving an authentic interpretation of the Word of God, whether in its written form or in the form of Tradition, has been entrusted to the living teaching office of the Church alone. Its authority in this matter is exercised in the name of Jesus Christ. Yet this Magisterium is not superior to the Word of God, but is its servant. It teaches only what has been handed on to it. At the divine command and with the help of the Holy Spirit, it listens to this devotedly, guards it with dedication and expounds it faithfully. All that it proposes for belief as being divinely revealed is drawn from this single deposit of faith.

It is clear, therefore, that, in the supremely wise arrangement of God, sacred Tradition, sacred Scripture and the Magisterium of the Church are so connected and associated that one of them cannot stand without the others. Working together, each in its own way under the action of the one Holy Spirit, they all contribute effectively to the salvation of souls.

III

PRIESTHOOD

Is a Baptized Man the Only Possible Valid Recipient of Holy Orders?

1. ". . . that the Church has no authority whatsoever to confer priestly ordination on women" (*Ordinatio sacerdotalis* 4)

1.1 *The* theological *right to the* question, *Why not?*

After the magisterial decision of Pope John Paul II in *Ordinatio sacerdotalis* (1994),[1] a gifted theology student, a woman loyal to the Church, was perplexed yet completely objective

[1] *Ordinatio sacerdotalis,* apostolic letter of Pope John Paul II "Reserving Priestly Ordination to Men Alone" (May 22, 1994), (Washington, D.C.: United States Catholic Conference, 1994); cf. also recent and important magisterial comments on this subject: *Inter insigniores*, Declaration of the Congregation for the Doctrine of the Faith on the Question of the Admission of Women to the Ministerial Priesthood (October 15, 1976), AAS 69 (1977): 98–116 [English bibliog.]; Pope John Paul II, Letter to Women (June 29, 1995), [English bibliog. The Latin text and English translation of all three documents can be found in: *From* "Inter Insigniores" *to* "Ordinatio Sacerdotalis": *Documents and Commentaries*, Congregation for the Doctrine of the Faith, preface by Tarcisio Bertoni, introduction by Joseph Ratzinger, commentaries by H. U. von Balthasar et al., (Washington D.C.: United States Catholic Conference, 1998)]; the German Bishops, "Zu Fragen der Stellung der Frau in Kirche und Gesellschaft" (September 21, 1981), published by the Secretariat of the German Bishops Conference (Die deutschen Bischöfe, 30). Theological commentaries have been collected and published in: Congregation for

63

in asking, "What do I lack as a woman, then, that I am supposed to be incapable of receiving the Sacrament of Holy Orders *validly*?"

Even though only a very small part of the world's female Catholics, in a Church with over a billion members, wonder about a vocation to the ministerial priesthood, many still feel deeply hurt by the statement that their status as women is considered the reason for their nonadmission to Holy Orders in principle.[2] Regardless of how the Sacrament

---

the Doctrine of the Faith, ed., *Dall'* "Inter insigniores" *all'* "Ordinatio sacerdotalis": *Documenti e commenti,* Documenti e studi, 6 (Vatican City, 1996).

[2] The Sacrament of Holy Orders is conferred in the degrees of bishop, presbyter, and deacon (LG 18–29). These should be distinguished from the earlier *ordines minores* (in the Latin Church), which do not form part of the Sacrament of Orders doctrinally but which, being ordered to the clergy, were connected with it *de iure ecclesiastico.* Tradition in its entirety firmly holds that all degrees of ordination are essentially rooted in one sacrament, as being a *repraesentatio Christi capitis* [representation of Christ the Head]. "Sacramentum ordinis est unum et idem pro universa ecclesia" [The Sacrament of Orders is one and the same for the universal Church] (*Trad. apost.* 3, 7, 8; Pope Innocent I, *Epistola* 2, 3; 25, 3; Gelasius I, *Epistola* 14, 6, DH 1326; 1601; 1766; 1773; 3857f.) There are various *ordinationes sacramenti* [ordinations within the sacrament] but not several *sacramenta ordinis* [sacraments of orders]. To the question of whether priesthood and diaconate are not only distinct degrees of ordination but also distinct sacraments, Thomas Aquinas replies (ST *Suppl.* 37, 1 ad 2): "The division of Order is not that of an integral whole into its parts, nor of a universal whole [into its genera], but of a potential whole, the nature of which is that the notion of the whole is found to be complete in one part, but in the others by some participation thereof. Thus it is here: for the entire fulness of the sacrament is in one Order, namely the priesthood [i.e., of the bishop or priest—Editor], while in the other sacraments there is a participation of Order" which, according to Thomas, is conferred and exercised in the two degrees of the episcopacy and the presbyterate. The bishop is the "princeps sacerdotum" [chief priest] and possesses the "apex sacerdotii" [the summit of priestly power] (*Suppl.* 40, 4), and therefore the priestly authority is vested in

of Holy Orders ought to be understood upon closer inspection: it still seems to many people today, inside and outside the Church, that the nonadmission of women to the Catholic priestly ministry is a final bastion of a millennium-long discrimination against women.

The Church's teaching

According to the Pope's formulation, we are dealing with a "matter of great importance . . . which pertains to the Church's divine constitution itself". Therefore every Catholic Christian has a right to find out what real basis there is in the "substance of the Sacrament of Holy Orders" (DH 1728; 3857), which even the Church's Magisterium cannot alter, for the statement that the Church (in the person of the bishop) *cannot* confer Holy Orders upon baptized women who live in complete union with the Catholic Church, even if she wanted to. The bishop's hands are tied, and not only by a canonical, disciplinary precept. Theologically this means that in the event that a sacramental rite was carried out in such circumstances, there would be no spiritual or sacramental effect on the "recipient" and the ordination would be invalid in God's sight.[3]

---

the bishop "sicut in origine, non autem in sacerdote, quia ipse non confert illos ordines" [as their source, but not in the priest, for he does not confer those Orders] (*Suppl.* 40, 7; cf. SCG 4, 76.).

Of a completely different nature, theologically and canonically, is the apostolate of all Christian believers, from which follows their "capacity of being appointed by the hierarchy to some ecclesiastical offices with a view to a spiritual end" (LG 33). It goes without saying that these "ecclesiastical offices" (director of religious education, etc.) are exercised by men as well as by women.

[3] Joseph Cardinal Ratzinger, the prefect of the Congregation for the

This, naturally, presupposes that the intrinsic reason for
the limits to the Church's activity is found in the *founda-*

Faith, in *Salt of the Earth: Christianity and the Catholic Church at the End
of the Millennium* (Stuttgart, 1996; Eng. trans.: Ignatius Press, 1997, p.
209), specifies the degree of binding authority of *Ordinatio sacerdotalis* by
saying that it is an act of the ordinary Magisterium to which infallibility
is attributed, as explained in *Lumen gentium*: "The bishops . . . proclaim
infallibly the doctrine of Christ . . . when preserving amongst themselves and with Peter's successor the bond of communion, in their authoritative teaching concerning faith and morals, they are in agreement
that a particular teaching is to be held definitively and absolutely" (LG
25). Cf. J. Ratzinger, "Grenzen kirchlicher Vollmacht: Das neue Doku-
ment von Papst Johannes Paul II. zur Frage der Frauenordination", IKaZ
23 (1994): 337–45, 338: The key sentence of OS reads: "[Wishing to
remain faithful to the Lord's example], 'the Church does not consider
herself authorized to admit women to priestly ordination.' In this statement the Church's Magisterium professes the primacy of obedience and
the limits of ecclesiastical authority: The Church and her Magisterium
have authority not in and of themselves, but rather from the Lord alone.
The believing Church reads the Scriptures and lives them out not as
some sort of historical reconstruction, but in the living fellowship of
the people of God in every age; she knows that she is bound by a will
that preceded her, by an act of 'institution'. This prevenient will, the
will of Christ, is expressed in her case by the appointing of the Twelve."
As a bridge between *Inter insigniores* (1976) and *Ordinatio sacerdotalis*
(1994) we find the following passage from *Mulieris dignitatem* (1988):
"Since Christ, in instituting the Eucharist, linked it in such an explicit
way to the priestly service of the Apostles, it is legitimate to conclude
that he thereby wished to express the relationship between man and
woman, between what is 'feminine' and what is 'masculine.' It is a relationship willed by God both in the mystery of creation and in the mystery of Redemption. It is the Eucharist above all that expresses the re-
demptive act of Christ the Bridegroom towards the Church the Bride.
This is clear and unambiguous when the sacramental ministry of the
Eucharist, in which the priest acts '*in persona Christi*', is performed by
a man. This explanation confirms the teaching of the Declaration *Inter
Insigniores*, published at the behest of Paul VI in response to the question concerning the admission of women to the ministerial priesthood"
(MD 26).

tional intention of Jesus.[4] This foundational intention is the reference point for the legitimacy of any and all ecclesiastical action. Of course it is not a formal legal precept and does not have to be traced verbatim to an explicit saying and command of Jesus in the New Testament. It arises from the sacramental nature of the Church, which is established in the revelation-event and which has made itself explicit in the history of her beliefs. We can demonstrate the foundational intention of Jesus by an orderly hermeneutic procedure using the normative sources of theology (Sacred Scripture, the doctrinal tradition and sacramental practice of the Church). It is the task of theology, in obedience to the sole authority in the Church—God's Word revealed in Jesus of Nazareth—to elucidate the intrinsic meaning of this foundational intention. The will of Christ is identical to the decision of the Logos with respect to us. It goes without saying that the authority of the foundational intention does not extend as far as it may seem in light of more or less evident arguments from reason. It may be that certain oft-cited suitability arguments from the tradition of Scholastic theology prove to be no longer convincing today; nevertheless this does not invalidate the recognition and acknowledgment of the foundational intention to which the *faith* tradition unanimously testifies.

---

[4] Cf. Ratzinger, "Grenzen kirchlicher Vollmacht", p. 337: "When Scripture, independently from the living tradition, is read in a purely historical way, the concept of *institution* loses something and is no longer obvious. Then the emergence of the priesthood no longer seems to be the recognition and acknowledgment of Christ's will in the developing Church, but rather appears as a historical process, preceded by no clear foundational intention, which therefore in principle could also have taken a different course. In this way the criterion of *institution* practically disappears and can be replaced by the criterion of functionality."

Thus there is justification for asking about the *real reason* [*Realgrund* = basis in reality] why women cannot receive Holy Orders.[5]

Even though no Catholic can make an individual claim to a sacramental ordination, this does not make Holy Orders something that the bishop can confer arbitrarily. Since he himself does not own Christ's authority outright but is only a servant appointed to transmit it sacramentally—"configured to Christ the priest in such a way that [he is] able to act in the person of Christ the Head [of the Church]" (PO 2), i.e., in proclaiming the Word, administering the sacraments, and shepherding the flock, he must carry out the Sacrament of Holy Orders in the way demanded by the nature of the priestly ministry and according to the Church's intention in administering the sacraments. There is no such thing as a litigious right to this sacrament; this is certainly not ex-

[5] The arguments that are proposed contrary to the perennial practice of the Church and the position taken by the Church's Magisterium can be found in: Ida Raming, *Der Ausschluss der Frau vom priesterlichen Amt: Gottgewollte Tradition oder Diskriminierung?* (Cologne/Vienna, 1973); Elisabeth Gössmann and Dietmar Bader, eds., *Warum keine Ordination der Frau?* (Munich/Zürich, 1987); Wolfgang Beinert, "Dogmatische Überlegungen zum Thema Priestertum der Frau", ThQ 173 (1993): 186–204; Peter Hünermann, "Lehramtliche Dokumente zur Frauenordination: Analyse und Gewichtung", ThQ 173 (1993): 205–18. Volume 3 (1993) of ThQ was a dossier on this subject; the contributions appeared also as a book: Walter Gross, ed., *Frauenordination: Stand der Diskussion in der katholischen Kirche* (Munich, 1996). See also Ernst Dassmann et al., eds., *Projekttag Frauenordination* (Bonn, 1997). Peter Hünermann, Albert Biesinger, Marianne Heimbach-Steins, Anne Jensen, eds., *Diakonat: Ein Amt für Frauen in der Kirche—Ein frauengerechtes Amt* (Ostfildern, 1997). An incomplete survey of the historical source material, which is interpreted according to the schematic assumption that there was a decline "from full, equal rights for women in the time of Jesus and the early Church to the increasing, socially conditioned misogyny of the Church Fathers and the Scholastics" is given by Friedrich Heiler, *Die Frau in den Religionen der Menschheit* (Berlin/New York, 1976), pp. 87–186.

plained by an arbitrary right of refusal on the part of the legitimate minister of the sacrament; rather it can only result from the structure and intrinsic meaning of the sacrament itself, which proceeds from the foundational intention of Jesus.

The connection between the Church's duty to administer the sacraments and the right to receive the sacraments can be demonstrated by means of another example: A baptized man and a baptized woman have no legal right to the Sacrament of Matrimony if the requirements for the valid reception of the sacrament are not present. If all the requirements are fulfilled, however, and the intention is there to do what the Church understands marriage to involve, then there is no right to deny a church wedding. Thus the argument that "women who feel called [to the priesthood] are not being discriminated against or excluded, because neither a man nor a woman has an individual and absolute right to the Sacrament of Holy Orders" is inadequate. For an individual's qualifications are not at issue here, but rather the basic theological understanding of this sacrament.

Correctly framed, the question is: whether *in general* the male sex of the candidate for the noble office of overseeing and caring for God's Church (cf. 1 Tim 3:5) is actually a requirement for the *valid* reception of the sacrament.

Difficulties in understanding

It shows little insight into the function of theology to try to reason that the fundamental rights enshrined in the constitutions of democratic nations (e.g., the citizen's rights to life and to freedom from discrimination on account of religion, race, or sex) could be the grounds for a legal claim upon the Church for the conferral of Holy Orders. The analogy does not hold, inasmuch as human rights per se are are not subject to positive law; besides, there is no such thing as a legal claim to be elected a member of parliament by the "sovereign people".

Arguments about whether or not women can be ordained priests must be drawn from the sacramental constitution of the Church and not from secular constitutional law—certainly not from positive law.

The difficulties in understanding this are more deeply rooted. In keeping with her faith-based understanding of Jesus' foundational intention, the *Ecclesia catholica* has had a tradition of conferring Holy Orders (which historically developed from the apostolic ministry in the early Church) only upon baptized males who as individuals had the requisite qualifications. This indubitably unanimous and consistent tradition is confronted, however, with the epoch-making transformation in psychological and social attitudes and with the everyday circumstances now affecting the co-existence of the two sexes in the governmental, economic, and cultural realms. More specifically, this contradiction is also evident in the change of self-image that women experience with respect to their own bodies and in their relations to the family (father, husband, children) and to the business world. There is to a large extent a comprehensive presence of women in public life. At least in Western civilization (Western Europe and North America), women can see their new feeling of self-worth affirmed every day in career-related successes and public acclamation.

"Emancipation" is perceived by everyone as a paramount social trend toward a normal state of affairs, a mighty movement that no one can oppose without exposing himself as a reactionary.

A new horizon of experience

A lack of trust in the capabilities of women, resulting from traditional roles and stereotypes, certainly cannot support the Church's position.

Any theology professor at a German university knows that the female students are in no way inferior to their male colleagues with regard to intellectual ability, spiritual vocation, and personal qualifications for ecclesiastical office, or in their dedication to the Church and to the gospel. New attitudes have developed. Young men, who from grade school through college have had no problems growing up together with girls, feel that it is an injustice when women are discriminated against in their opportunities for advancement and when they are not *allowed* to take up a profession that they *want* to pursue. Furthermore, there is not the slightest reason to fear that the women theology students, on average, would be any less capable of dealing with the psychological, physical, or spiritual demands of pastoral ministry.

A glance at everyday reality in the parishes shows to what extent the Church, especially in Africa, Asia, and Latin America, was built and continues to be built up through the services of women. In many areas of evangelization, catechesis, pastoral care, and administration, ecclesiastical life would be considerably impaired without the honorary and official ministry of women. The face that the Church presents to the world is much more feminine than the slogan about a "male-dominated Church" would lead you to suspect.

Hence the conferral of Holy Orders upon male recipients cannot be explained by pointing out some alleged "unsuitability" that goes with being a woman. In many countries, furthermore, Catholics can see for themselves the work of female Lutheran pastors (when participating in ecumenical worship services, joint church weddings, funerals, etc.). Regardless of the momentous difference in their understanding of ministry, of which only very few have a theological awareness, the thought occurs: "Why shouldn't it be just like that with us?"[6]

So the question unavoidably arises whether the actual presence and importance of women (evident since the Church's origins) in all areas within the Church and in all fields of the Church's missionary activity does not demand *today*, at long last, their admission to *all* offices and ministries as well.

The equality and equal rights of women today permeate all departments of life, leave their mark on societal attitudes, and shape the beliefs and thinking of individuals and groups; this state of affairs demands that the Church, for the sake of her credibility, resolutely turn her back on a practice that only reflects a preenlightened, as yet unliberated anthropology and sociology and that—so the reasoning goes—is only being carried around like a burdensome foreign body within modern society.

If the "Church in the modern world" would only interpret the "signs of the times" correctly (GS 4, 11), the argu-

---

[6] From an ecumenical perspective, it should become clear at last, in view of the common practice and doctrinal belief of Catholics and Orthodox with respect to the sacramentality of the priesthood and the admission of men only as candidates, that *theological* arguments are required here. Thus, the more emotional considerations are of little help ("I can't imagine a woman at the altar"; "I dream that some day my granddaughters will be able to become priestesses"). Furthermore a purely pragmatic justification (deference to the Eastern Churches, fear of schism by traditionalists) is insufficient, because such situations involving church polity can change. The ecumenical unity of the Church cannot be built upon external similarities alone, but rather must be rooted in a greater fidelity to the gospel and the truth that it contains.

ment continues, she could take her place at the forefront of social progress. By putting into action in her own internal organization the ideal that she extols in her social teaching, the Church could become a model for the new collaboration of men and women in society. She would open up for herself and for society all the riches of female gifts and talents. Besides this, the Church has the prerogative, they say, of reforming and reshaping her spiritual ministry in every age according to the needs of modern evangelization and pastoral care. No doubt spiritual ministry belongs to the very essence of the Church, but the Church can do more about it than she thinks she can.

In terms of pastoral strategy, also, the effect of this new openness supposedly would be enormous. Women, too, could then identify in a new way with "their" Church, once the "structural discrimination" against women and their categorical exclusion from spiritual ministry had finally been overcome.

The search for the correct hermeneutic

The hermeneutic that we have just summarized briefly is not directly theological in its approach but is informed instead by sociological models and schemata of liberation; this sort of hermeneutic, of course, discovers its own limitations when it is applied to "the mystery of the holy Church[, which] is already brought to light in the way it was founded" (LG 5). For what the Church is and should do is manifested only in faith and in listening to the Word of God. It is precisely in the sacraments that the Church recognizes the absolute autonomy [*Unverfügbarkeit* = *indisponibilité*, Fr.] of revelation and the limits of human competence [*Gestaltungsrechts*]. The Church of God cannot decide to "market" herself as the man-made model of a liberated utopian society or as the prototype of liberal anthropology, just for the sake of advertising or improving her image. Neither her internal nor her external activities can be measured by the standard of a societal order organized from the top down, or of a liberal-democratic constitution founded upon the idea of equality. For the "hierarchy" is not the rule of clerics over the Church, but rather "sacred authority" [ἱερά ἀρχή]. Inasmuch as the One who sends is himself represented in those sent [the apostles, ἀπόστολοι], this authority is exercised by Christ as the "origin" (Head) of all salvific activity in the Church. The presence and collaboration of the laity, which is an *essential* part of the Church, is not the result of adopting democratic elements but rather follows from their Baptism and their membership in the Church.

The important thing is to rediscover what the Church *is*, by reflecting on the mystery of her origin in God's eschatological communication of himself in Jesus Christ, the Word of God made flesh. The Church, in Christ, is "the sign and instrument" (LG 1) of the reign of God, which has begun and which is being accomplished dynamically in history.

God has willed to save men, not as individuals, but as a people (LG 9). In this sense the Church may also be an example of justice and solidarity in society, without becoming a societal subsystem herself, and without making her visible form a photocopy of the contemporary structure of society.

The Church is the *communion of all believers* originating in the Word of God, which is built up internally through her charisms, works of service, and the ministries of teaching and governing in the name of Christ, the Prophet, Priest, and Shepherd—ministries that God himself has granted to her in the Sacrament of Holy Orders. Only as such can she do justice to her mission as the "sacrament of salvation" for the world in Jesus Christ.

1.2 *The right to a* theological answer

Once we get past the unproductive dispute over who bears the burden of proof, we should emphasize that believing women and men have the *right* to a *theological* answer to the question of whether the Church's practice is based on the inner logic of the Sacrament of Holy Orders or is merely the reflection of a sociological and anthropological disregard for women that therefore, in principle, can be changed.

For the question, after all, is this: Can it be that the Church, conditioned by nontheological influences, has not applied fully her *own* principles in this matter of Holy Orders? Creation theology provides a basis for the doctrine that woman has full and equal dignity as a person, and the theology of grace applies this principle in examining the ways in which baptized women are related to God and to the Church (membership in the Body of Christ). From the very beginning the Church has also let these principles come to the fore without restriction in her practice of Baptism, Confirmation, Reconciliation, the Anointing of the Sick, and Matrimony.[7]

The discussion to date, both before and after the magisterial decision in *Ordinatio sacerdotalis*, has proved the necessity of insisting that the question be framed at the *theological* level. The danger of subordinating the theological explanation of revelation to some other norm should not be dismissed lightly.

In the context of a pluralistic society, the Church appears to many outsiders and non-Catholic believers (and to many

[7] Cf. GS 29 and John Paul II, Letter to Women (June 29, 1995).

who are estranged from the Church) mainly as a sort of religious subsystem or as a free alliance of men and women, who join together on the basis of their emotional-religious and ethical convictions and thus "form their own church". People imagine that the Church's form of organization is something analogous to that of political parties, labor unions, co-ops, banks, or political action committees. Even those who do not share the Church's self-understanding—that she has a divine origin and serves as an instrument of God's universal salvific will—still think that they are justified (as can be seen over and over again) in offering constructive criticisms, or that it is their job to demand the application of societal standards and values within the Church, for example, democratic procedures, equal opportunities for advancement in all capacities and offices, etc. In such cases the Sacrament of Holy Orders, at any rate, is considered to be little more than a Baroque or antiquarian form of appointment to a position of leadership, like that of a bank president, party chief, industrial magnate, television station manager, or university professor—a position in society that can be pinpointed on-screen according to calibrated readings of self-fulfillment, career chances, power (i.e., "having the final say"), or prestige.

In an atmosphere resulting from a secularized understanding of reality and a reductive, functionalist view of man, it is clearly difficult to find common ground so as to initiate a dialogue—based on God's communication of himself, mediated historically through the Incarnation—about the sacramental understanding of the Church in her works of service, charisms, and ministries, as well as about the image of man that is rooted in theological anthropology, an image characterized essentially by the mutuality of man and woman.

The Church, however, cannot make decisions on doctrinal questions and in sacramental theology with a view to the anticipated effect on public relations, i.e., to reducing tensions between intra-ecclesial convictions and societal attitudes. The Church cannot be guided, like a political party, by voting trends and opinion polls and change into a new outfit accordingly. The appropriate forms for internal dialogue about doctrinal questions in a Church that understands herself to be the *communio of believers* are yet to be found, as far as the constraints of the mass media are concerned. Anyone who is not willing to bend and break others in order to have his ideas prevail realizes that he is obliged to participate in an objective exchange of opinions. Besides, the Church is much closer to a democracy (which is not only a form of government but also a philosophy of life) than she is to any authoritarian and ideological form of wielding power, provided that one does not reduce the essence of democracy to majority rule and the defense of minority rights but rather grasps the fact that democracy is based on the recognition of fundamental rights (analogous to the *ius divinum*), which are by definition beyond the purview of positive legislation (analogous to the *ius ecclesiasticum*).

The source of teaching authority and the basis for decisions in doctrinal questions, however, are found neither in the Magisterium itself (as a court of appeal established for sociological reasons, in the false sense of "hierarchy") nor in "democratic, consultative" panels of priests and laity, but rather in the Word of God and in the Church's faith, which springs from the Word and presents itself as the expression of the Word in human language. Listening results in understanding, by faith, the *foundational intention of Jesus*, the Mediator between God and men (1 Tim 2:4f.), the Head of the Church and the Source of the new humanity (Eph 1:22; Col 1:18; Rom 5:17, 19).

The questions that must be treated here—questions of sacramental theology and theological anthropology about the nature and mission of the Church and questions about the binding force of doctrinal decisions—are so weighty that it is not permissible to give an evasive answer in an effort to buy time. It makes even less sense to go a step farther and expect the "solution" to come from the Holy Spirit in the distant future. In contrast to this rather transcendentalist view of the Spirit's action, we should recall the inner unity of Pneumatology, Christology, and ecclesiology. The glorified Christ works in the Holy Spirit without bypassing historical causality (Scripture, tradition, the hermeneutic for explaining revelation, the *sensus fidei* of the People of God, the Magisterium). Rather, the working of the Spirit ensures that the human articulation of revelation remains what it is supposed to be, namely, the actualization [making-present, *Vergegenwärtigung*] of the Word and will (1 Thess 2:13) of the God who has revealed himself once and for all in Jesus (Heb 10:10).

Likewise in the future, the Spirit of God, who guides the Church, is not going to settle questions pertaining to dogma by handing down messages from heaven, or solve contemporary problems by bringing about historical coincidences like a *deus ex machina*. The Spirit always works, rather, *through* the historical transmission of revelation in Scripture and tradition. He works through the *sensus fidei* of the Church as a whole and through the teaching authority of the episcopacy. There is no way of bypassing the concrete, historical circumstances in which the Church's doctrines are put into practice; the coherence of these creaturely forms and the final results depend on the Holy Spirit (cf. Jn 14:16, 26; Acts 15:28).[8]

---

[8] The rather formal discussion about the degree of binding force possessed by *Ordinatio sacerdotalis* is necessary for a precise understanding of the document but does very little to elucidate the subject matter. The alternatives cannot be the false dichotomy: either "infallible" (in which case it must be accepted even without any insight into the reasons for the decision, or despite a recognition that the decision does not do justice to the matter) or "fallible" (in which case *Ordinatio sacerdotalis* is nothing more than an opinion of the Pope as a private person, no different

Therefore the decisive question is as follows:

Is there a reason for the consistent praxis Ecclesiae *and the traditional belief that the candidate must be of the male sex in order to receive the Sacrament of Holy Orders validly that lies in the sacramental character of the priestly ministry, or does this belief (and hence the practice) prove, in light of contemporary sociology and anthropology, to be historically conditioned and thus only incidentally connected with the Sacrament of Orders?*

We should add, though:

The question of "theological necessity or sociological conditioning" cannot be evaluated according to sociological parameters, but must be decided solely and exclusively by theology.

from any other theological statement). Even if *Ordinatio sacerdotalis* were an *ex cathedra* decision, the justification for the contents of the doctrinal statement would have to be theologically evident or be made evident from Scripture and tradition. An understanding of magisterial decisions as arbitrary would in no way do justice to the connection between the substantive authority of the Word of God and its reception in the Church's obedience of faith. Cf. Manfred Hauke, "*Ordinatio sacerdotalis*: Das päpstliche Schreiben zum Frauenpriestertum im Spiegel der Diskussion", *Forum Katholische Theologie* 11 (1995): 270–98; Norbert Lüdecke, "Also doch ein Dogma? Fragen zum Verbindlichkeitsanspruch der Lehre über die Unmöglichkeit der Priesterweihe für Frauen aus kanonistischer Perspektive", TThZ 105 (1996): 161–211; Leo Scheffczyk, "Das responsum der Glaubenskongregation zur Ordinationsfrage und eine theologische Replik", Forum Katholische Theologie 12 (1996): 127–33; Jean-Pierre Torrell, "Note sur l'herméneutique des documents du magistère: À propos de l'autorité d'Ordinatio sacerdotalis", FZPhTh 44 (1997): 176–94; German trans.: "Die Verbindlichkeit von *Ordinatio sacerdotalis*: Zur Hermeneutik lehramtlicher Dokumente", in Gerhard Ludwig Müller, ed., *Frauen in der Kirche: Eigensein und Mitverantwortung* (Würzburg, 1999), pp. 357–79.

*The unconditional character of the faith and
the historical limitations of plausibility*

The fact that the theological comprehension and formulation of the meaning of revelation is at all times conditioned, in its own expression, by individual and collective epistemological presuppositions, which can be historical, philosophical, and psycho-social, is a consequence of the fact that revelation is conveyed to men through human forms of communication. Revelation is always "God's word in the mouths of men" (cf. I Thess 2:13). In order to determine more precisely, under new and different circumstances, the relationship between the absolute character of the *content* of faith and the conditional character of its articulation in the *profession* of faith, we must refer back to the historico-theological hermeneutic of the Catholic faith.

One cannot regard (or "expose") the articles of faith as being in every respect dependent upon and determined by group interests or pathological psycho-social obsessions, be they of an individual or collective sort. The incessant parade in the twentieth century of intellectual fashions, hard-and-fast ideologies, and absolutist practices, extending to the tyranny of public opinion, admonishes us to be careful about identifying the majority position of the moment with the truth per se, or to believe that the truth automatically comes to light with the passage of time. One can not merely inquire about the sociological and psychological conditioning of particular articles of faith, considered only as to their material object. Ever since Kant, no one can assume the vantage point of epistemological naïveté and overlook the inevitability of critical reflection on and questions about the knowing subject's own conditioning, as evident in his criteria, his value judgments, and his motives.

Every socio-philosophical constellation is a synthesis of ultimate, basic beliefs and the empirical conditions for their realization. The modern agenda of equal rights and equal opportunity for women has its deepest foundation in the Christian belief in the equal dignity of man and woman, as persons, before God and in relation to each other, a belief enshrined in creation theology and the theology of grace. The doctrine of an ontic or essential inferiority of woman would be clearly heretical, since it is diametrically opposed to the revealed testimony as to the goodness of creation (Gen 1:31). This basic belief has undergone a variety of emphases within the framework of changing sociological conditions, and a definitive equilibrium will never be reached. In the conditions brought on by a high-technology civilization, the presence of women takes a different form in all societal accomplishments, just as the role of men, too, is changing.

The anthropology that is founded in revelation is not identical with the cultural, social situation of the relationship between men and women in a particular epoch of Church history. This anthropology can be actualized, critically and constructively, even under the much-changed social and intellectual conditions of the industrial age and the age of communications.

Altering the *contents* of this anthropology, however, leads to a functionalist view of man, in which it is not a question of the societal and ecclesial presence and participation of women and men, but rather a matter of reducing fundamental personal relations (woman relating to man as to her father, husband, son, brother) to a functional level (the fatherless society, the woman's loss of her maternal identity, the absence of a basic, formative experience of marriage and family, the distortion of sexuality, which is a means of personal self-giving and unity, into self-gratification). A functionalist anthropology results, historically, from the modern dualism that misunderstands the corporeality of man, likening it to a psycho-physical mechanism and attributing to the bodiless soul an ahistoric, idealized sort of being.

In view of the different contents of these two anthropologies—the one personalist and holistic, the other dualistic and functionalist yet accompanied by horrible dysfunctions—the relation between theological anthropology and sacramental theology, on the one hand, and the social and cultural status quo, on the other, cannot be defined and interpreted by uncritically adapting the Christian view of man to prevailing standards.

A Christian who wants to be intellectually accountable for his faith will address the specific question from sacramental theology—whether the male sex is an essential prerequisite for the valid reception of the Sacrament of Holy Orders—within the context of a comprehensive, historico-theological hermeneutic of the Church's sacramental character.

This reference to the sacramental character of the Church and of the priesthood does not yet contain the final answer to the question, whether the priestly ministry can be validly conferred only upon a baptized male; it does indicate, however, the level at which the answer is to be sought and found.

2. ". . . pertains to the Church's divine constitution" (*Ordinatio sacerdotalis* 4)

The Pope situates the magisterial decision on the current question, whether the Church can *validly* confer Holy Orders upon baptized women, within the framework of the Church's divine constitution; in so doing he highlights a fundamental principle of theological hermeneutics.[9]

[9] Peter Hünermann's attempt ("Lehramtliche Dokumente zur Frauenordination: Analyse und Gewichtung", ThQ 173 [1993]: 205–18; "Theologische Argumente für die Diakonatsweihe von Frauen", in Hünermann, *Diakonat*, pp. 98–128) to pull the rug out from under the magisterial decision in *Ordinatio sacerdotalis* and also *Inter insigniores* with

2.1 *The historico-theological hermeneutic of the*
Catholic faith

The Church understands herself to be related to Christ in a
way unlike the relationship of any other religious institution

---

the observation that the arguments set forth there are unconvincing to
him personally will seem more than odd from the perspective of a Catholic conception of theological epistemology. The practice of the faith
that is based on Scripture and tradition, and also the speculative elucidation of it emerging from the essence of the Sacrament of Orders as
the representation of Christ, the Head of the Church, cannot be rendered relative by means of sociological arguments. Only a justification
in keeping with the sources and criteria of theology could prove to be an
adequate basis for a change. Until now the "vote" for a departure from
the consistent practice of the Church is based solely on the mere *conjec-
ture* that sociological and anthropological notions about the inferiority
of women determined the procedures followed by Jesus and the ecclesiastical authorities from the very beginning. There is no proof that the
Church's beliefs until now with regard to the Sacrament of Holy Orders
followed from such an axiom. There is no doubt whatsoever that the
notion of a biological inferiority or a "theological" second-class status
of woman, insofar as she is a human creature, is in principle incompatible with the Catholic faith. Furthermore it is certain that such notions
belong, rather, to Gnosticism or are the product of certain philosophies
of emanation, in which the idea of creation (and thus of the personal
immediacy between God and man) is unknown.

In the case of a conflict between the Magisterium and the personal
opinion of an individual theologian (who has the backing of slogans and
trends publicized in the media), the latter cannot really lay claim to the
ultimate judgment, over and above the Magisterium. How this alleged
superiority of theological opinions over the Magisterium is to be reconciled with the epistemology of Catholic theology, as it most recently
has been set forth again in *Dei Verbum*, remains a riddle. The arguments
that Peter Hünermann has proposed in his contribution, "Theological
Arguments for the Diaconal Ordination of Women", do not address the
"Theological Misgivings about the Diaconal Ordination of Women"
expressed by Hans Jorissen in the same anthology (i.e., magisterial documents, the justification based on the unity of Order, and the witness of
tradition). In no respect can such arguments diminish the force of these

to its historically remote founding figure. Just as God's communication of himself in Jesus Christ is ultimately unique and unparalleled, so too is the Church, as the communion of believers, unique and irreducible to any other societal structure. Therefore she cannot take her organizational structure from society and its subsystems.

The Church, as the communion of faith and of believers, owes her existence instead to obedient listening to the Word of God, encountered historically in Jesus of Nazareth. Jesus Christ, being true God, the Eternal Word who has communicated himself in becoming flesh, reveals himself as the real, historical foundation for the Church's existence, communion, and mission. In the power of his Spirit, who has been poured out in the final age, he brings forth the visible form of the Church in the unity of her mission and the multiplicity of her works, offices, and charisms, in such manner that the Church's sacramental essence is manifested and made really present in her visible form.

Harking back to the theology of the sacraments, which ultimately are rooted in Christ's Incarnation, Cross, and Resurrection, Vatican II gave new prominence to *sacramentality* as the decisive organizational principle of the Church. The sign character of the sacraments participates in the reality of the real communication of grace and illustrates it visibly and audibly in the realm of man's sensory experience:

---

misgivings. If the Church had in fact been in error about a question that concerns her divine constitution, the sacraments, and the fundamental data of anthropology (the equal personal dignity of all men), then her sacramental structure would be undermined and the connection between historical revelation and its faithful transmission in tradition would be destroyed; at best she would be able to hold meetings as a group of Jesus-supporters.

The one mediator, Christ, established and ever sustains here on earth his holy Church, the community of faith, hope and charity, as a visible organization through which he communicates truth and grace to all men. But, the society structured with hierarchical organs [i.e., the episcopal, presbyteral, and diaconal ministries; cf. LG 20] and the mystical body of Christ, the visible society and the spiritual community, the earthly Church and the Church endowed with heavenly riches, are not to be thought of as two realities. On the contrary, they form one complex reality which comes together from a human and a divine element. (LG 8)

The teaching authority of the bishops as successors to the apostles is bound up with the contents of revelation, which are manifested in Scripture and tradition, the place, so to speak, where revelation is explained in the Church's beliefs. This magisterial mission springs from the historical event of God's communication of himself and constitutes an essential moment in the historical perpetuation of that communication in the ongoing experience of the Church as the community of those who hear the Word. Since this teaching authority remains strictly determined by revelation, it can do no more than make accessible the contents of revelation in their individual elements and aspects—a process carried on by the Holy Spirit himself. Magisterial decisions are binding interpretations of revelation and hence, with regard to their force and structure, *analytical judgments*. They participate in the absolute, nonarbitrary character of the act of faith and of the Church's profession of faith, inasmuch as the determination found in this human profession is an outward sign or icon of God's determination on behalf of mankind, in which the former is rooted.

The divine constitution of the Church, therefore, is not the product of historical data, apprehended in a positivistic way, about the individual regulations, teachings, or ethical precepts of Jesus before his Resurrection, as was assumed by a methodology oriented to the isolated sayings of Jesus. Jesus did not appear on the scene as one figure of religious enlightenment among many others. He revealed himself as the authoritative Mediator of the Kingdom of God in the final age, a dominion that is established in the world through the destiny of the "only Son from the Father" (Jn 1:14, 18) in the Cross and Resurrection.

The consequence of all this for believers is that Jesus, even though his human consciousness was molded by the intellectual climate of his time, did not and could not err in the institutional acts by which he established the reign of God and founded the eschatological People of God. To assume here a dependence of Jesus upon his age that obscured the truth of revelation and that then was fully recognized only in light of the most recent scientific and sociological findings would be tantamount to depriving Christianity of its historical basis in revelation.

An immanentist or secularist perspective (e.g., of the school of comparative religion) categorically excludes any recognition of God's Word revealing itself in human language and in the community of hearers and believers. Such a viewpoint will instead dismiss as an ideological construct any utterance of God about himself that is conveyed to the understanding of believers by means of human words as well as historical phenomena and events. According to this perspective, any ideological construct can be "deconstructed" or exposed, in terms of the history of religion, psychology, or sociology, through an analysis of the human factors and elements that brought it about.

2.2 *The sacramental character of the Church as the foundation for historical doctrinal decisions*

On the other hand, once the act of faith is made, which is an effect of the Holy Spirit's communication of himself so that we might understand the Word of God in Christ, the divine constitution of the Church is seen to be the sacramental actualization of God's communion with men, which is rooted in the incarnation of God in Jesus Christ. This divine constitution is set forth and realized in the historical salvific mission of Jesus, in his work of gathering the People of God, and in his destiny as the Mediator of salvation by his Cross and Resurrection, in the presence of his Spirit, and in his Parousia.

Thus the declaration of the *hypostatic union*, for example, is not the result of elaborating on the notion of a relationship to Jesus that was originally simple and emotional, or of grasping his "meaning for us" in general categories such as "ethical model", "catalyst of religious, romantic yearnings", or "guru". Rather, it is only the common linguistic expression for something that is comprehended in the original faith-understanding of the apostles: the union, maintained by God himself, of the *Word* of his eschatological and incarnational self-revelation for the salvation of all mankind with the *human* Mediator of this same salvation, which is God himself.

Likewise, when the early Church recognized the *universality of Jesus' mission for the salvation of all men*, this was not due to a saying of Jesus that was suddenly remembered, but rather to the insight, made possible and maintained by the Holy Spirit of the glorified Lord, that God's forgiving and life-giving affirmation of all men has taken place in Jesus and that Israel's election is now fulfilled in the addition of those who believe in Jesus, the Christ of all, now that God has made the Church "of Jews and Greeks" to be a "sacrament—a sign and instrument, that is, of communion with God and of unity among all men" (LG 1).

Likewise, when the Church, in the course of unfolding and formulating her faith through the ages, came to realize that seven of the fundamental acts she is authorized to perform not only symbolize salvation, but also really and concretely impart that salvation to the recipient when the symbolic act is carried out, then it was not an arbitrarily broader or narrower definition of terminology that was decisive in recognizing the *sacramentality of the seven sacraments*, but rather the recognition of a real characteristic, common to and informing all these symbolic actions that was now conceptually represented by the precise term "sacrament", for the purposes of verbal agreement within the faith community.

Likewise, when after several disputes the Church finally and definitively arrived at the recognition of the *validity of Baptism administered outside of full communion with the Catholic Church*, this cannot be traced back in a purely positivistic way to sayings of Jesus or instructions of the apostles. It resulted from the insight into the sacramental essence of Baptism. In order to justify this conclusion, which is of great ecclesiological and pastoral importance, it is naturally assumed that the essence of Baptism can be determined from the original testimony of revelation in Scripture and in the fundamental acts that the Church is authorized to perform.

The dimension of historical development and concretization can be observed in all questions of Church doctrine, in the liturgy, and in the mission and structure of the Church. This by no means compels us to subscribe to a relativism that results from the (systematic) juxtaposition of suprahistorical, essential truths, and random historical facts. The truth of God reveals itself *in* the event of its proclamation, which unites the mind and the will of the listener with God, who is the content and horizon of man's truth and freedom. Therefore the truth of revelation and the historicity of its transmission are not in opposition, but rather intrinsically interrelated.

This historical form of handing on tradition is based on the historical structure of revelation itself. The transmission of divine revelation in the evangelization and life of the Church can take place in no other way than in the reciprocal interaction of fidelity to the *deposit of faith* and the *actualization* of the gospel in an ever-new hearing of both the Word of God in Sacred Scripture and of its interpretation in tradition. In this process the Church does not receive any new revelation, concrete instructions, or theological data—for example, how the sacramentality of Baptism and Confirmation are to be distinguished from one another. The fact that Baptism is unrepeatable cannot be proved by a saying of Jesus. But it follows objectively from the fact that Baptism is the death of the old man and rebirth to everlasting life.

In this process of arriving at an agreement within the Church, the decision-making authority confronts a contemporary question while remaining, itself, bound to uphold the testimony of Scripture; therefore one cannot postulate that this competent authority has a preternatural basis or is per se in need of justification. The decision is entrusted to men, with their human means. There is only one way of taking into account the incarnational character of revelation: the fact that God's Word is declared in human words and communications and that the declaratory intention of this Word is determined to be something already given with reference to a particular question. That way is by means of a conscientious human decision, according to the best historical and theological knowledge available, and with the help of the Spirit that was promised to the Church.

Thus Vatican II formulates the task of the apostolic teaching authority, the exercise of which is entrusted to the bishops, as the ultimate and binding decision wherein the unequivocal nature of God's Word is expressed with regard to a particular problem.

> But the task of giving an authentic interpretation of the Word of God, whether in its written form or in the form of Tradition, has been entrusted to the living teaching office of the Church alone. Its authority in this matter is exercised in the

name of Jesus Christ. Yet this Magisterium is not superior
to the Word of God, but is its servant. It teaches only what
has been handed on to it. At the divine command and with
the help of the Holy Spirit, it listens to this devotedly, guards
it with dedication and expounds it faithfully. All that it proposes for belief as being divinely revealed is drawn from this
single deposit of faith. (DV 10)

2.3 Is the person of the recipient part of the "essence of the Sacrament of Holy Orders"?

Since, according to the Catholic understanding, the priestly
ministry is based on the sacramental nature of the Church
and of her mission, specifically represents it, and proves to be
one of the fundamental, sacramental acts that she authorizes,
the question about the recipient (and the rightful minister)
pertains to the essence of the Sacrament of Holy Orders. In
pointing out the sacramentality of priestly ordination, we
reach the level at which the reasoning pro and con must
take place. Not functionality, but *sacramentality* is the decisive criterion for all theological argumentation.

For the Christian ecclesial communities that know only of a difference of function or of degree between the common priesthood of all
the faithful and the office of the ordained ministers of the Word, the
liturgy, and pastoral duties (bishop, priest, deacon), no particularly
theological problem arises, at most a pragmatic one. For if the minister
[*Amtsträger*] is merely someone who is officially called and receives
a mandate to perform a ministry that is already conferred upon all
the community members, then there is no objective reason whatsoever that baptized women cannot exercise the priestly ministry of the
community. For the Catholic (and the Orthodox) Church, both the
distinction between the common priesthood and the ordained priesthood and also the justification for the ordained priesthood as a specific
participation in the priesthood of Jesus Christ (and thus the impossibility of deriving it from the common priesthood) are constitutive

elements in the sacramental understanding of the nature and mission of the Church; therefore an attempt to draw a parallel between the Catholic priestly ministry and the ministry of the Lutheran pastor—which is open to women, too—is theologically unconvincing. The agreement between the Catholic Church and the Orthodox Church in their teaching that a man is the valid recipient of ordination is rooted, not in an external traditionalism, but in their firm belief in the sacramental character of Holy Orders.

At the same time it is important to note the psychological dimension and the normative force of an actual practice, which leads not a few people to ask, "If women can become pastors in the Lutheran Church, why shouldn't it be possible in our Church as well?" In this connection one should refer to the ecumenical efforts to reach a common understanding of ministry. However true it may be that ecumenical dialogue is necessary and that one should remain open to different positions in the other ecclesial communities, the discussion within the Catholic Church about the recipient of the Sacrament of Holy Orders can be conducted only within the framework of an explicitly sacramental theology.

Anyone who considers the Church to be merely a community of like-minded individuals, which is structured according to the general socio-psychological laws studied in the history of religions, or who mistakes Catholic ordination to the priesthood for the sort of solemn ceremony by which the "officials" of a religious community are installed in office or hierophants are designated to serve their deities, will find incomprehensible and puzzling the meaning and scope of arguments based on the sacramentality of the Church.

In the present intellectual climate, the question about the possibility of priestly ordination for woman becomes entangled with the question of whether one can find a biblical basis at all for a sacramental priesthood. For those who have a functionalist understanding of ministry, this problem does not exist.

What does "the essence of a sacrament" mean?

By the essence of a sacrament is meant the inner (invisible) grace (*res sacramenti*), which is made evident to the senses and re-presented in the outward signs by which the sacrament is administered (*sacramentum tantum*). The spiritual content of the sacrament, in any case, is not something that the Church is competent to modify in any way. This is true also for the sacramental sign (liturgical words, constitutive symbolic actions, and material signs), when it goes back to Jesus himself or when it is clearly recognizable in the practice of the early Church and historically has left a mark on the liturgical ceremonies. As part of the *substantia sacramenti*, some of the sacraments have a lasting effect (*res et sacramentum*), either in the recipient (*character sacramentalis*) or in the sacramental signs (the Real Presence of Christ in the consecrated eucharistic gifts).

Baptism, Confirmation, Holy Orders, and Matrimony bring about in the recipient a relationship to Christ the Head of the Church and to Christ whose Body (as a social structure) is the Church. This relationship to Christ and to one's fellow Christians marks the person who receives these sacraments with a permanent character (*character sacramentalis indelebilis*). Baptism and Confirmation effect a communication of sanctifying grace that makes the individual a member of Christ's Body and a full participant in the supernatural life of the triune God. On the other hand, priestly Orders and Matrimony confer a special grace that enables the priest to carry out the ministry entrusted to him with the authority of Christ for the salvation of the faithful, or else that enables the husband and wife to live a married life in such a way that it portrays the loving union of Christ and the Church, a union in which Christian marriage shares and from which it acquires its significance as the common path of the two partners in their grace-filled communion with God.

The difference between man and woman as an essential element in the Sacrament of Matrimony

Two elements in the lasting effect of the Sacrament of *Matrimony* (*res et sacramentum*) are the ongoing participation in the union of Christ with his Church and the representation of the loving covenant of Christ (as Bridegroom, Head) and the Church (as his Bride and his Body). Thus the essence of the Sacrament of Matrimony is found not only in the wedding liturgy but also in the ongoing relationship between the husband and the wife. This correlation of different and irreplaceable ties between one person and another is founded upon the sign-character of masculinity and femininity; through this natural symbolism spouses open their hearts to one another in love and devotion.

Persons who marry actually are the sacramental sign of Matrimony for each other, inasmuch as they consummate the sacrament as husband and wife in the essential marital act. In their life for one another is portrayed the life of Christ for the Church and the Church's response in the life of the husband for his wife and of the wife for her husband.

The Latin-rite wedding liturgy formulates it correctly: "I take you as *my wife*" or "as *my husband*", and not some abstract, asexual expression such as "my partner in life". Therefore the sexual difference between man and woman, which makes them complementary in a specific way, is a constitutive element in the Sacrament of Matrimony. Between husband and wife there is, not a symmetry of equality, but rather a symmetry of difference. This symmetry does not consist in an equality of the phenomenological or ontological, essential sort, but rather in the personal mutuality of man and woman, which has as its foundation the distinctive value and distinctive reality of masculinity and femininity. The lover can communicate himself to the other only through his being different. Being sexually different is the one thing that makes *fruitfulness* of love possible (in mutual assistance and in the child of both spouses).

For this reason, even prior to any moral or aesthetic considerations, a woman *cannot* receive the Sacrament of Matrimony with a woman, and for the same reason a man *cannot* receive the Sacrament of Matrimony with a man. The loving covenant of Christ with the Church is supposed to be manifested in the grace of Matrimony, which brings about a participation therein; in a unisex partnership, however, which lacks the natural relation of the sacramental signs, there would be no basis for that grace. This incapacity does not entail any discrimination or denial of a possibility that could be for a person's good; it simply manifests a fundamental given of creation, that woman was created *for* man (1 Cor 11:9, which is certainly not the same as saying "for man's sake"), and that man "shall . . . be joined to his wife, and the two shall become one [flesh]" (Eph 5:31; cf. Gen 2:24; Mk 10:8). For "*in the Lord* woman is not independent of man nor man of woman; for as woman was made from man, so man is now born of woman. And all things are *from God*" (1 Cor 11:11; emphasis added).

*The relatedness of man and woman as an essential
element in the sacramental sign of priesthood*

One of the lasting effects of *priestly ordination* is that the ordained man henceforth can act with the *authority* of Christ, because, by virtue of their commission, Christ makes himself present and acts in his messengers (Mt 28:19; Lk 10:16; Jn 20:21; 1 Clement 42–44; LG 20). This inner reality of Holy Orders is expressed in the circumstance that the ordained man, in his *person* and in the relation of man to woman symbolized in human corporeality, represents and symbolically manifests the personal relationship of Christ, the Head, to his Church. Only in the personal *mutuality* of husband and wife and in their personal *communion* can the mutuality and unity of Jesus Christ and the Church become tangible. The incarnate Logos, through his devoted surrender of himself, has become one flesh with the Church, his Bride, i.e., has entered into a common life with her. In this respect the symbolism of "man to woman and woman to man", which God inscribed in his creatures, provides the possibility for a revelation of God's covenant with his people and—as the perfect realization thereof in the "fullness of time" (Gal 4:4) —for the sacramental unity of Christ and Church in "one Person", "in one flesh".

Therefore the essence of the Sacrament of Holy Orders, which is a given, prior to any ecclesiastical competence to interpret or modify it, includes not only the conferral of authority to proclaim the gospel, to sanctify in the administration of the sacraments, and to exercise the pastoral ministry of Christ. To the essence of Holy Orders belongs also the ordained man, who in his person represents Christ in his fundamental relation to the Church.

> In the person of the bishops, then, to whom the priests render assistance, the Lord Jesus Christ, supreme high priest, is present in the midst of the faithful . . . in such wise that bishops, in a resplendent and visible manner (*eminenti ac adspectabili modo*), take the place of Christ himself, teacher, shepherd and priest, and act as his representatives (*in eius persona*). (LG 21)

Among the several ways in which Christ is present in his Church, the Council expressly mentions his sacramental presence "in the *person*" of the man who carries out the priestly ministry (SC 7, emphasis added).

The conferral of power and authority constitutes the grace of the Sacrament of Holy Orders (*res sacramenti*). The sign of imposing hands and the prayer of ordination make the ordained man—in his person, which is the consequence of his being a soul-body composite—a representative of Christ (*res et sacramentum*). The ability to be such a representative presupposes the natural symbolism of human life in the correlation of man and woman.

If priestly ordination consisted only in the conferral of the power and authority to act as minister of the Word and of the sacraments and to lead the Church, then it would be superfluous to ask whether the holder of this authority is qualified to be a *sign* of the specific relation of Christ to his Church, based on the natural symbolism of the sexual difference between man and woman.

2.4 *Anthropological notes on the difference between the sexes*

To make this clear, an anthropological reflection on the difference between the sexes, having its origin and basis in the act of creation, proves to be indispensable. Even though this difference cannot be pinned down to one particular characteristic, an exclusive social role, etc., this does not demonstrate that an anthropology of masculinity and femininity is irrelevant, but only that man is a mystery eluding hasty and all-too-easy attempts at definition. Still, there can be no reasonable doubt about the importance of the fact that man was created male and female (Gen 1:28), the significance of which pervades every department of human life: spiritual, physical, historical, and social.

Corporeality as the archetypal sign in human communication

Man as a person becomes accessible to his fellow man only within the sign of his corporeality.

Symbols, in the strict sense, are not conventional tokens but rather spring from the being that God has communicated to all creaturely realities, a being that they show forth and make present by way of analogy, each in the measure of its participation in the source of Being. In this sense, every existing thing (to the extent that its nature permits) is an appearance, a manifestation, and thereby a symbolic representation of Being and, thus, a form conveying the perception of God's invisible reality, everlasting power, and divinity in the works of his creation (Rom 1:20; Wis 13:1–9; Acts 17:24–29).

Splitting off empirical knowledge of reality in the objectivity of "things" from a symbolic or subjective interpretation thereof, i.e., "loading" things with what they mean "for me", would be the end of all theology (e.g., arbitrarily ascribing to the death of Jesus on the Cross a salvific meaning that Jesus could not and did not know of or intend).

Only on the basis of the analogy of being and of knowledge can God's revelation, expressed in its worldly medium, dawn upon man's mind. The symbol is rooted in what is symbolized. Man as a creature is a structural unit of symbol and thing symbolized: he is mind, which knows God and to which God can and does make himself known, in the creaturely mediation of the "image of God".

With reference to the anthropology of man and woman, this means that personal self-realization finds expression, in keeping with human nature, within the range of possibility afforded by the body. The body is the concrete symbol of the soul. In actualizing himself as a soul-body composite, one human person symbol-izes, that is, makes himself present for the other. The body is the medium for the complete communication of self to another person and for full communion with the other.

Marriage is the foundation for man's social existence (diachronically [throughout history] and synchronically [at a given moment]) and, at the same time, its unsurpassable expression. If sexuality is an essential characteristic of the body, then the difference between man and woman is part of being human; hence this difference manifests itself as the archetypal symbol of interpersonal communication in love and also proves to be the fundamental idea in the mediation of incarnational, sacramental salvation.

Marriage as the archetypal symbol of God's covenant with Israel/the Church

Therefore to talk about Yahweh's marriage covenant with Israel and the union of the Church as Bride with Christ her Head, so as to make "one person" (Gal 3:28; Eph 2:15; 5:31f.), is not merely to use a superficial metaphor. A reality is revealed and accomplished here in a symbol that is rooted in creation (anthropology) and in the covenant event. Precisely for this reason, this language about the marital bond "Yahweh-Israel" and about the Bridegroom-Bride relationship between "Christ and the Church" cannot be replaced by or derived from any other imagery.

According to a binding article of faith, human nature is fully realized in both sexes. This truth also includes, though, the insight that the human person is actualized *in* a nature

that is sexually determined (and not apart from that speci-
fication) and that the human person transcends self in ap-
proaching another person. That is why the human person
is, per se, irrevocably open to marital and familial life. As
is evident in marriage, man is ordered to community; this
is the natural "sign" upon which the sacramentality of the
Church builds. "[God] has, however, willed to make men
holy and save them, not as individuals without any bond or
link between them, but rather to make them into a people"
(LG 9).

The Christian way of life described as "celibacy for the sake of the
Kingdom of Heaven" has nothing to do with denying personal self-
fulfillment, understood sexually, but rather is the symbolic representation of Christ's selfless relationship to the Church, God's family
and, thus, an expression of concern for the "affairs of the Lord", that
is, the salvation of the faithful (cf. 1 Cor 7:32ff.; Mt 19:12). Christian celibacy does not dwell somewhere beyond the basic polarity of
human existence; rather it is a particular way of realizing the marital
nature of human existence. The difference between male and female,
in which man's *creaturely* existence is manifested, thus does not consist
of an inferiority in the case of the allegedly weaker sex. Rather, this
difference is a positive expression of an underlying truth that can be
believed and acknowledged only when the world is understood as
Creation, i.e., as a share in Being that is granted by God and thus as
a showing-forth of God's unconditional affirmation of his personal
creatures.[10]

Since God created man as male and female, the showing-
forth of his dominion is symbolically realized in different but

[10] Cf. Hanna-Barbara Gerl-Falkovitz, "Es lebe doch der Unterschied?
—Zum Spannungsfeld Frau und Mann im Christentum", in Gerhard
Ludwig Müller, ed., *Aufbruch ins Dritte Jahrtausend: Theologisches Arbeits-
buch*, Auf dem Weg zum Heiligen Jahr 2000, vol. 2 (Cologne, 1997), pp.
351–83. The Gnostic talk about God having a composite, masculine-
feminine nature, or likening the relations of Father, Word, and Spirit to
those of husband-wife-child, was opposed by Gregory Nazianzen (*Fifth
Theological Oration*, 8) and Augustine (*De Trinitate*, 12, 5f.), among others.

related ways in a man and in a woman. This is evident in their different and yet inseparable tasks when using the gift of human fertility to produce offspring and in their respective duties in cultivating the world (Gen 1:27). The disturbance in man's relationship to God through original sin is inherited and manifests itself in diminished social relations between man and woman and in the increased difficulty of living up to their original callings, which follow from being a man and being a woman (Gen 3:14–19).

It is not possible to speak of an enmity between man and woman. That is put between the woman and the "serpent", while Adam "knows" his wife, that is, lovingly becomes one flesh with her. Their offspring proceed from this *love*. For this reason he calls her "Eve" (life). She becomes the mother of all the living (Gen 3:20) and thus the effective sign of God's life-giving power (in nature and grace) against that power which is the enemy of life.

The Church Fathers, of one mind with Sacred Scripture, have recognized the "great *sign* [that] appeared in the heaven: a *woman*" (Rev 12:1, Douay Rheims; emphasis added) as referring to the Church and Mary. Through her faith, Mary becomes "the mother of [the] Lord" (Lk 1:43). The Church proceeds from him. Just as death came through both sexes, so too should life come through Christ, the new Adam and progenitor of the new human race, as well as through Mary, the new mother of the living (the Eve-Mary parallel).[11]

---

[11] Irenaeus of Lyons, *Adversus haereses*, 3, 22, 4; Augustine, *Sermo* 140; Epiphanius of Salamis, *Haer.* 78, 18. In more precise terms, Erik Peterson observes (*Der Brief an die Römer,* Ausgewählte Schriften 6, ed. Barbara Nichtweiss [Würzburg, 1997], p. 132): "The essential element in original sin is the fall of Adam, and not the seduction of Eve. . . . This distinction is called for because of the different metaphysical position of the man with respect to the woman in the order of creation. As a consequence of this distinction, Paul said in 1 Corinthians 11:3 that Christ

The unity and diversity of man and woman "in Christ"

When Paul goes so far as to interpret the relationship between man and woman within marriage in light of the trinitarian and soteriological relation of Father and Son in the
communio of the Spirit and speaks of the wife as the reflected
glory of the husband [I Cor 11:7], it is not a question of
theological embroidering upon contemporary social circumstances affecting the marital partnership between man and
woman.[12] It is certainly not meant as a sweeping generaliza-
tion about the way "men" and "women" live together in society.

Just as the trinitarian relationship of Father and Son is
characterized by neither subordination nor inferiority on
the part of the Son, but rather marks a procession within
the Deity, whereby the Son is "in the form of God" and
equal to the Father (Phil 2:6), so too husband and wife have
"one nature" because they share equally in God's image. God
the Father is the origin (I Cor 11:3: "the head of Christ is
God") of the soteriological mission of the Son. When the
Son, obedient even to death on the Cross, accomplishes his

---

is the Head of every man, while the husband is the head of his wife.
These categorical distinctions between man and woman, between Adam
and Eve, are metaphysically determined and cannot be dismissed; they
may not be dismissed any more than the distinction between Jews and
Gentiles. If one does so anyway, it destroys human nature. Because the
man fell, we can only be redeemed likewise by a man. Christ became
not only a human being, but a man. Just as Eve only participated in
the Fall, so too can the woman cooperate in our redemption only by
way of participation. Only in this passive, participatory sense, then, is
it possible to contrast Mary and Eve."
[12] Cf. Christoph Schönborn, *God's Human Face: The Christ Icon* (San
Francisco: Ignatius Press, 1994), pp. 8–14, on the christological and
trinitarian transformation of the Hellenistic concept of "image".

task, God's glory begins to shine in the human face of Christ
(2 Cor 4:6).

When the husband—imitating that loving devotion that
leads to self-emptying and obeying the divine command to
be an image of the *kenosis* of the Son of God—empties himself, too, of all self-love, desire to dominate, self-sufficiency,
and airs of superiority, then he is the reflected glory and the
image of God according to the standard of Christ, who in
his obedience to the Father is God's image. The husband
is designated head of his wife, not for the sake of theologically legitimizing a relation of dominance, but in order to
align the husband's conduct with the mind of Christ, who
by virtue of his mission (as Head of the Church) loved the
Church and gave himself up for her, so as to become "one
flesh" (= a loving union) with her (Eph 5:25).

Thus the countenance of the wife should glow with the
reflected light of her husband's love. In the mutual self-giving
of their love, the two spouses portray in their self-emptying,
which is always for the sake of the other, the irrevocable character of the relation between God and man. Both spouses,
personally and in their marital union, are representatives (as a
unity of head and body, original glory and reflected glory):
they are an image and likeness of the love of God being
poured out on men in Christ. This profuse love is the power
of God's dominion, for he rules as Creator and Redeemer
while granting a limitless share in his Being and in his communion of love within the Trinity.

In the mystery of sacramental marriage is revealed the
most profound significance of the fact that man is made in
the image and likeness of God; as husband and wife, man
symbolizes God's dominion, as the source of created being
in the uncreated Love of God (= the Love manifested in his
dominion). Christ is the Lord of the *basileia* [kingdom] of

God, but not by analogy with a secular ruler who conquers a realm for himself. He is the *Kyrios* by virtue of his *kenosis* and his obedience to the revelation of the glory of God the Father, a glory that is reflected in the salvation of mankind (cf. Phil 2:6–11).

Woman (a wife) is described as "the glory of man" (1 Cor 11:7) and symbolically represents, in her natural relation to man (her husband), the bridal response of faith and love made by the Church, which Christ by his devotion has made into his Body. (Cf. 1 Cor 11:10, "That is why a woman ought to have a veil [ἐξουσίαν, *potestatem* = (sign of) authority] on her head.") Such language here, however, is by no means an attempt to legitimize social subordination (despite the frequent misuse of quotations from the Bible as arguments in the battle between the sexes), to give an ideological justification for a particular social "role", or to prove any sort of biological or essential inferiority. The standard for the ethical conduct of spouses is mutual subordination, whereby they both take as their spiritual model the obedience of Christ, who in his fidelity to the Father subordinated himself to the logic of his mission. The subordination of the wife to her husband is a criterion based, not on societal conditions, but rather on the subordination of the faithful to Christ (Eph 5:22: "Wives, be subject to your husbands, as to the *Lord*"; emphasis added).[13]

In the logic of the vocation to marriage, what follows

---

[13] The Christian understanding of the father and husband is characterized, not only by a fundamental restriction of the ancient Roman idea of *patria potestas* [fatherly authority], but also by the new definition of headship, not as *dominatio,* but as *caritas coniugalis* [spousal love]. Cf. Ambrose, *Hexaem.* 5, 7, 18f.; Basil the Great, *Hom. in Ps.* 1:3; John Chrysostom, *Hom. in Gen.* 45:2; *In 1 Cor.* 19:1, 26:8; *In Eph.* 20:2; Augustine, *De bono conj.* 7; *Contra Faustum* 19, 26; 23, 8; *Serm.* 51, 13; *De nuptiis et concupiscentia* 1, 10, 17, 21.

from the husband's obedience to Christ is precisely not dominion over others, but rather the *kenosis* of love for his wife
and their children. The obedience of faith that the wife (as
a Christian) renders to Christ expresses itself in the obligation (*freely* undertaken) to remain faithful and to fulfill her
duties in marriage and in the family. This love, which opens
itself to the love of the husband (Col 3:18; 1 Pet 3:1–7),
is a symbolic manifestation of the free subordination of the
Church to Christ (and a participation therein), from which
arises a living communion with Christ. The real meaning of
this re-presentation can be grasped with precision only if we
consider that Christ did not subject himself to the Church,
but rather the Church submits to Christ in the obedience
of faith, i.e., acknowledges him as *Kyrios* (1 Cor 15:28; Phil
2:6–11).

The standard for this attitude is the *kenosis* of the *Kyrios*,
who subjected himself to the will of the Father so as to make
possible, in this sign of his perfect, unselfish love, an entirely
unforced self-surrender of human beings in the freedom of
faith and love. In the logic of a personal vocation, subjecting oneself to Christ leads to freedom in the Spirit (Gal 5:5)
and to that love which is not self-seeking but which rejoices
in the other's welfare (1 Cor 13:5f.). The *many* (men and
women), to whom the free gift of righteousness has been
granted abundantly in Baptism, "*reign* in life through the *one
man* Jesus Christ" (Rom 5:17; emphasis added).

In those passages where Paul is setting forth his reflections
—based on the theology of Creation and of the Covenant,
on Christology and on the theology of grace—about the personal equality of man and woman and the relational-symbolic
difference between them, which he manages to do without
reducing the symbolic difference to an abstract uniformity
or an unrelated juxtaposition, his argumentation is often

quite subtle and not always easy to understand. Thus commentators repeatedly have referred to the supposed tension between the two doctrines elucidated above (which are only comprehensible in a christological and trinitarian context), namely: (1) the teaching about the "mutual subordination of wife and husband in a common reverence for Christ" (cf. Eph 5:21), and (2) the statement in Galatians 3:26–28: "[F]or in Christ Jesus you are all sons of God, through faith. For as many of you as were baptized into Christ have put on Christ. There is neither Jew nor Greek, there is neither slave nor free, there is neither male nor female; for you are all one in Christ Jesus." Upon careful inspection, nevertheless, this tension is resolved. For Paul is speaking to the Galatians in connection with the theology of Baptism, reasoning that the difference between Jews and Gentiles in salvation history, the difference between slaves and freemen in society, and the sexual differentiation between man and woman present no obstacle to the fullness of divine adoption for all believers in Christ: because of the union of Head and members in Christ, all are "one".

Even though Paul refers to the radical symbolism of man and woman simultaneously in terms of Christology, ecclesiology, and the theology of marriage, he does not end up contradicting himself. This is because the difference between male and female, which has its origins in creation and through which the image of God in man manifests itself, is not something relative (in contrast to sociological conditions), but rather is continually reestablished and perfected in its original positivity. Men and women *both* are immediately related to God. Marital partnership, though, is an image of the eschatological *communio* of God with mankind in love. This partnership represents the bond between Christ (as Head) and the Church, and from this representation it acquires its orientation toward the *mysterium* of Matrimony, which can be completely elucidated only by theology.

The symbolic representing of Christ, the new Adam, in the priest's masculinity

One element belonging to the essence of the Sacrament of Holy Orders is the sign-value in the person (and not merely in the authority) of Christ's representative, who portrays his relation as the Head and Bridegroom to the Church as his Body or his Bride. This being the case, priesthood as a sacrament is inherently concerned with the natural symbolic structure of creation, which expresses itself in the differentiation and interrelation of man and woman. The man who is ordained a priest is, in his person and by reason of his nature (as a human being in the significant relation of man to woman and thus with a disposition to fatherhood), a sign through which Christ, the High Priest, accomplishes the life-giving actions of his Church. Therefore the spirituality of the priest cannot be reduced to a few pious exercises that enable him to proclaim the gospel somewhat more credibly. Priestly spirituality consists essentially of being conformed to the way of life, the mind, and the fate of the crucified and risen Lord.[14] This, of course, is true in various ways for all the sacraments, and in the case of Holy Orders specifically it means taking on Christ's way of life, so as to be able to act sacramentally, symbolically, and effectively in the person of Christ as Head of the Church.

> Because it is joined with the episcopal order the office of
> priests shares in the authority by which Christ himself builds

---

[14] Cf. Leo Scheffczyk, "Der Zölibat als integraler Bestandteil der christusförmigen Existenz des Priesters", in Klaus M. Becker and Jürgen Eberle, eds., *Der Zölibat des Priesters*, Sinn und Sendung, vol. 9 (St. Ottilien, 1995), pp. 19–43.

up and sanctifies and rules his Body. Hence the priesthood of priests, while presupposing the sacraments of initiation, is nevertheless conferred by its own particular sacrament. Through that sacrament priests by the anointing of the Holy Spirit are signed with a special character and so are configured to Christ the priest in such a way that they are able to act in the person of Christ the head. (PO 2)

3. Systematic exposition of "the teaching that priestly ordination is to be reserved to men alone"

3.1 *The Incarnation of the Word in the man Jesus of Nazareth: Christ as Bridegroom of the Church*

"God became man" and took on human nature in the masculine mode. The WORD reveals itself in the FLESH of Christ Jesus as the "only SON of the Father" (Jn 1:14, 18, 41, 49; emphasis added), who by virtue of giving his flesh for the life of the world (Jn 6:51) is the Bridegroom of the Bride (Jn 3:29), namely, the Church.

Although in Christian faith we call the Divine Persons Father, Son, and Spirit, we cannot infer from this that they have a masculine or feminine nature (inasmuch as *ruach* in the Old Testament is in most cases grammatically feminine). For God perfects his nature above and beyond the sexual characteristics of his creatures. Father, Son, and Spirit are the bearers of God's act of being-in-relation, who in an analogous manner of speaking are designated by their relations of origin. God's paternal or maternal actions toward men in love, grace, and providence are "appropriated" to one or another of the Divine Persons but pertain to each of them. In contrast to the biblical understanding, the Gnostics recognize both masculine and feminine redeemer figures and imagine God as a sort of family.[15]

[15] Cf. Hans-Josef Klauck, *Die religiöse Umwelt des Urchristentums II. Herrscher- und Kaiserkult, Philosophie und Gnosis* (Stuttgart/Berlin/Cologne, 1996), p. 177: "Theoretically, Sophia can also creep into Gnosticism in the role of the heavenly messenger; the redeemer figure is then fitted

When the eternal Word of God becomes flesh, it assumes humanity in one of the two sexes. For man, considered as a flesh-and-blood entity, is a concrete, individual human being as a male or a female (Gen 1:27, 2:23f.). *Included* in this anthropological understanding is the relatedness of one human being to another, which manifests itself in the difference between the sexes, not as a restriction, but as something positively beneficial (Gen 1:27: "[M]ale and female he created them"; Gen 2:24: "[T]hey become one flesh").

Since the human nature of Christ does not remain something external to the Person of the eternal Son of God, it cannot be exchanged for another sort, not even hypothetically. Although God was free with regard to the *fact* and the *manner* of the Incarnation, one still cannot conclude from the contingency of this event that the sex that was assumed, the historical period, the place, and the circumstances in salvation history (within the horizons of Israel) were arbitrary and might have been otherwise. God certainly did not allow the conditions and the thought patterns of the time to determine his actions, as though reasoning that the *Verbum incarnatum in natura humana masculina* would have a greater chance of success in a patriarchal society. The Incarnation proceeds from God's sovereign free will and takes place within the basic anthropological parameters inscribed in his creation as a manifestation of his wisdom and goodness (Wis 13:1–9; Rom

---

out with feminine traits [or alternatively with the notion that she has a masculine partner—GLM]. . . . *Protennoia* means "first thought" or, to use a better, feminine word, "the first Idea". She is what the father-god thinks first, before all time and above all worlds, and she contains the feminine aspects of his nature. Her own first word, her *logos*, is considered at the same time to be her son. The result is the trinity of father-mother-and-son, which is not that rare in Gnosticism." Christian anthropology knows nothing of a patriarchal view of mankind, which admits woman only as a diminished actualization of human nature. The biblical faith in God did not arise from a projection onto the deity of a particular view of humanity or of human interpersonal relationships; hence the God of the Christian faith is neither an absolute monarch, nor a patriarch, nor a man, nor a fellowship of a man, a woman, and their children.

1:20). Where the basic anthropological data are obscured by sin and dysfunctional structures, the anthropology of man's new life in Christ provides the standard for social and cultural arrangements, and not vice versa.

In John's Gospel the line of communication is clearly set up as follows: Jesus Christ (1:18), being the incarnate WORD (1:1, 14), is the only-begotten SON of the Father (1:14) and the BRIDEGROOM of the Church (3:29; cf. Rev 19:7; 21:2; see also Mt 9:15; 2 Cor 11:2; Eph 5:21–32).[16]

The masculinity of Jesus is part of the Logos' self-expression in the flesh and forms the basis for the original relation of Christ to the Church and for his sacramental union with her as *his* Body and *his* Bride.

Through the natural symbolism of the sexes, God communicates the reality of his free, historical, and corporeal presence in the world. By assuming humanity in the mode of masculinity, the Logos communicates himself in his dealings with the new people of God in that fundamental personal relationship that has its foundation in masculinity.

Thus the Dogmatic Constitution on the Church of Vatican II can say: "Christ loves the Church as his bride, having been established as the model of a man loving his wife as his own body (cf. Eph 5:25–28); the Church, in her turn, is

---

[16] Cf. Karl-Heinz Menke, *Fleisch geworden aus Maria. Die Geschichte Israels und der Marienglaube der Kirche* (Regensburg, 1999), esp. pp. 45–55. The bridegroom-bride symbolism, therefore, is by no means a mere metaphor used to illustrate an objective state of affairs. Rather, the relation of bride and bridegroom in the human sphere is based on God's real gift to mankind. In the Bridegroom-Bride relationship of Christ and the Church, the real, salvific connection between Christ and the Church becomes visible at the symbolic level and opens up to the believer and the lover a real fellowship with Christ and, thus, a participation in the most intimate communion of men with God and of human beings among themselves (cf. LG 1–4, 9). Cf. Sara Butler, "The Priest as Sacrament of Christ the Bridegroom", *Worship* 66 (1992): 498–517.

subject to her head (Eph 5:23–24). 'Because in him dwells all the fullness of the Godhead bodily' (Col 2:9)" (LG 7).

Inasmuch as the capacity for interpersonal relationships is realized in sexually determined human nature, masculinity (potentially) results in the fundamental human relationships to a son/daughter, a wife, a brother/sister, and a father/mother. These personal relationships, in which personhood is realized in its most radical, anthropological sense, constitute a reality quite distinct from the functional relationships to a neighbor, colleague, or schoolmate, however friendly or beneficial the latter connections may be.

It is significant that, in biblical testimony, God's relationship, as Creator of the world and Founder of the covenant, to the members of the People of God is always expressed symbolically by means of the primary personal relations essential to being human. Consequently Christ, as the incarnate Word, is the only begotten *Son*, in whom the glory of the *Father* makes itself visible, audible, comprehensible, and communicable (Jn 1:14–18; 1 Jn 1:1–3). Anyone who believes in his message and follows the way of Christ "is his *brother*, and *sister*, and *mother*" (Mk 3:35; emphasis added).

To understand such sayings requires more than an essential or ontological determination of the relation between man and woman. In their case it cannot be a matter of two entities brought into being independently of one another, who are juxtaposed on a secondary level as "having equal rights" and are then compared to each other quantitatively from various points of view (sociological, psychological, legal). Since man and woman are fundamentally bound up with each other in their common human nature, the sexual difference in their actualization of human nature is the constant and inexhaustible source of the positive character of the relational capacity inherent in personhood. The differentiation in their sexual existence as man or woman does *not* mean *a demeaning dependency*, but rather—on account of the positive character of the difference—*a love that builds up and affirms.* The equal dignity and equal rights of a person before God and as a member of the Body of Christ, the Church, do not come about in some hypothetical realm beyond the sexual difference, but rather *within* this difference and *through* it. Masculinity and femininity cannot be reduced one to the other; each has a unique value; the insight into the positive character of the difference, in which this value comes to light, would be distorted by a mind-set that remained under the spell of a dualistic metaphysics of the Cartesian sort. According to that view, the corporeal substance of man, which can be explained by the laws of a psycho-physical mechanism, is only accidentally connected with an asexual conscious substance. An anthropology of this sort abolishes the foundation for any discourse about the incarnational, sacramental self-communication of God. Viewed historically, such a concept resulted also in a truncated, moralistic "cultural Christianity". It then became impossible for the priest to represent Christ in his person and in his way of life. His ministry was reduced to the rhetorical art of furnishing the consciousness of Christians with religious doctrine and inculcating moral views.

As opposed to a dualistic anthropology (following that of René Descartes), the theological anthropology that develops upon a biblical foundation, with its holistic understanding of man as a body-soul composite and its insight into the radical symbolism of the man-woman-difference, offers an important corrective. Therefore the sign-value of masculinity and femininity, which is bound up with the difference between the sexes, cannot simply be dismissed as a "symbolic" or "metaphorical" way of thinking, inferior to a theology oriented toward empirically tested data and historically verifiable facts and limited to subjective interpretations.[17]

[17] Augustine (*De Trinitate* 12, 13) rejects an explanation of the differentiation and association of man and woman that would rely on the Platonic schema of mind vs. sensuality. This cannot be reconciled with the Judeo-Christian doctrine of the image and likeness of God. Inasmuch as human nature consists of mind and sensuality, man and woman are created in the image of God and enter into an immediate personal relationship with God. Even the depiction of the creation of man and the

If Jesus Christ, according to his humanity, is the real symbol of God's *communio* with men, then in the symbol of his masculinity, i.e., in the inherent relatedness of man and woman as creatures, is also revealed God's free decision to bind himself to the chosen people of God as the fatherly Author of the covenant, as the Bridegroom of the bride Israel/Daughter Zion (Is 61:10; 62:5; Jer 2:32; Hos 2:20f.; Zeph 3:14).

As "the Son" (Mk 13:32), who addresses Yahweh as "ABBA, Father" (Mk 14:36; emphasis added), he is—from God's perspective—the eschatological representative of God. As Son, he became, however, with regard to Israel and mankind, the father of the race, the New Adam, the Head of the Church and the Head of the new humanity. Just as the "sonship" of Israel (Rom 9:4; Hos 11:1) has its origin in the patriarchs, the kings, and the messianic "Son of David" (cf. Mt 2:15) and is summed up in the form of a person, so too is Jesus Christ the origin of the divine sonship of all the faithful. He comprises all the members of his Body, of which he is the Head, in "one person" (cf. Gal 3:28; Eph 3:15). The Suffering Servant of God, who "makes himself an offering for sin, . . . shall see his offspring [and] prolong his days" (Is 53:10).

This specific relationship of "the one to the many" is ev-

---

creation of woman out of the man's rib shows that the woman is in fact one flesh with the man, so as to become one flesh with him in marriage. It was only an anecdote [i.e., not a serious theological controversy] that at the Council of Macon (585), according to the report of Gregory of Tours (*Hist. Franc.* 8, 20), a bishop who knew little Latin asked whether a woman can be referred to as *homo*. Thereupon the other participants in the synod explained to him the difference between *vir* and *homo* in Latin. From this incident developed the Scholastic question, "whether a woman has a soul". Cf. H. Leclercq's article, "*Femme*", in DACL 5/1 (1922), pp. 1349-53.

ident also in the selection of the twelve apostles to be the forefathers of the new covenant people and in the call of the seventy-two disciples to be representatives of the seventy-two nations of the world (Lk 10:1).

The Son who, in the human nature that he assumed, represents the Father (the Creator of the world, the Bridegroom of Israel, the Lord God of hosts), took on *flesh in the symbolism of masculinity* (Jn 1:14; 3:29; Mk 2:19f.; Lk 5:34f.; Mt 25:10), in order to become "one flesh" with the Church, which he won as his Bride by loving her and giving up his life for her. Just as a man leaves his father and mother so as to be joined to his wife, so too through the self-offering of Christ—the Lord, Shepherd, and Head of the Church, his Bride—all believers become members of his Body. They become one flesh and one Body with him, i.e., a community of life in love (Eph 5:21–33; 2 Cor 11:2; Rev 19:7; 21:2; 22:17; cf. also 2 Clement 14:2).

No privileged status for males can be deduced from all this, as is evident from the fact that "the Son of man also came not to be served but to serve, and to give his life as a ransom for many" (Mk 10:45). The husband as head of his wife is not the ruler, but the servant of his wife, just as Christ —in obedience as the One sent by the Father—became the Servant for the salvation of mankind.

3.2 The Church as the Bride of Christ: The communion of men and women in the Body of Christ, the Church

In the human nature united to himself, the son of God, by overcoming death through his own death and resurrection, redeemed man and changed him into a new creation (cf. Gal 6:15; 2 Cor 5:17). For by communicating his Spirit, Christ mystically constitutes as his body those brothers of his who

are called together from every nation. . . . He is the head of
the body which is the Church. . . . All the members must be
formed in his likeness, until Christ be formed in them (cf.
Gal 4:19). (LG 7)

The relation of Christ to the Church as his Bride is the
origin and perpetual basis of the common participation of
all the members of the Church in the priestly, kingly, and
prophetic ministry of Christ.

The call to communion with Christ in his Church is valid
for all human beings. Jesus is much more radical than any
social critic or world reformer, because he establishes a standard for evaluating interpersonal relations that is based, not
upon human interactions, but rather upon the interaction
of God with man. Men and women are equally creatures of
God and, by virtue of being made in his image and likeness,
representatives of his goodness. All of them, however, are
also subject to the destructive power of sin. Yet that is why
his saving works, which conquer sickness, human discord,
and death, are meant for *all*.

In Mary, his Mother (Lk 1:38; 2:51; 11:28) and in other
women (Lk 10:39; Jn 4:39) we find individuals and types
of discipleship in general who (with deep understanding)
are *hearers of the word of Jesus*. Sick women receive healing
from him by reason of their *faith* (Lk 7:50). Jesus (not at
all impressed by any casuistry, social circumstances, or intellectual constructs) returns radically to the will of God
expressed in creation by reestablishing marriage as the real
symbol of God's faithfulness and love toward mankind, despite all hardness of heart, i.e., the unwillingness of the inner
man to act according to the grace of God's covenant with
his people (Mk 10:3ff.).

The transformation of the company of disciples before
Easter into the paschal and Pentecostal "Church made up

of Jews and Gentiles" (cf. Eph 2:14) in no way detracts
from the call of all "men and women" (cf. Acts 17:4, 12)
to salvation and to full membership in the Church, which
is the People of God, the Body of Christ, and the Temple
of the Holy Spirit. All receive the Holy Spirit (Acts 2:17);
through Baptism all are drawn into Christ's filial relation
to the Father and are members of the Church in an unre-
stricted sense (Gal 3:28). They are "joint heirs of the grace
of life" (1 Pet 3:7) and, through their reception of the eucharistic gifts, form *"one* body" in Christ (1 Cor 10:16f.)
in the cooperation of his members with the *many* gifts of
grace, charisms, ministries, and works (1 Cor 12:4–6).

Baptized women, in the Spirit of God, are called to and
endowed with prophetic speech, i.e., so as to testify to their
knowledge in the faith for the edification of the congregation (1 Cor 11:5; Acts 21:9), to support the apostles and the
Christian communities (Rom 16:1–16; 1 Cor 16:19; Phil
4:3; Col 4:15; 2 Tim 4:19, 21; Acts 16:15), just as, before
Easter, some women accompanied Jesus and provided for
him and his disciples out of their means (cf. Lk 8:1–3). By
virtue of their Baptism they are appointed to serve the sick
and the needy (1 Tim 5:3–16; the enrolled widows), to give
witness, and to present the teaching of the faith, both inside (Acts 18:26) and outside the Church (Acts 17:4), to
instruct their (still nonbelieving) husbands (1 Cor 7:14ff.),
so that they, "though they do not obey the word, may be
won without a word by the behavior of their wives" (1 Pet
3:1). They should instruct their children (2 Tim 1:5) or,
through their exemplary way of life, teach younger women
what is good and *train* them (Tit 2:3–4; emphasis added;
cf. Prov 31:26). Timothy was schooled in the faith and pre-
pared for his apostolic ministry by his grandmother Lois and
his mother Eunice (2 Tim 1:5).

In contrast to early Gnostic tendencies within the congregations, the Church, true to the faith handed down from Paul (1 Tim 6:20), says that marriage is good, like everything created by God (1 Tim 4:3f.; cf. Gen 1:31), and that childbearing does not demean a woman by involving her with (supposedly evil) matter, but is rather an occasion for her to experience God's holiness (1 Tim 2:15) as a blessing for herself and the "fruit of [her] womb" (Lk 1:42). Whereas Gnostic groups admitted women to the ministries of teaching and governing ("ruling over one's husband"), the Catholic Church recognized that the ministry of the bishops and presbyters, who are men (1 Tim 3:2), is inseparably connected with being male (cf. also 1 Tim 2:12).

The fact that in the Gnostic groups women, too, functioned in positions of leadership (analogous to the episcopal and presbyteral offices) is not evidence of an early emancipation movement, but on the contrary is based on a disdain for the created difference between the sexes and for sexuality in general.[18]

---

[18] This is pointed out by Thomas Söding, "Mysterium fidei. Zur Auseinandersetzung mit der 'Gnosis' in den Pastoralbriefen", IKaZ 26 (1997): 502–24, n. 29 (responding to Kurt Rudolph, *Die Gnosis, Wesen und Geschichte einer spätantiken Religion,* UTB 1577, 3d ed. [1977; Göttingen, 1990], pp. 291ff.). The Montanist "prophetesses" Priscilla and Maximilla renounced their marriages. On the other hand, ecclesiastical writers, opposing the Gnostics, Marcion, the Encratites, and the Manichees, emphasize the meaning and legality of marriage and childbearing: Irenaeus, *Adversus Haereses* 1, 24, 2; Hippolytus, *Ref.* 7, 28, 20; Methodius of Olympus, *Sympos.* 2, 2; Augustine, *De bono conj.* 33; *Haer.* 46, 13; Synod of Braga, DH 461; Fourth Lateran Council, DH 802, 916. When dogmatic distinctions are made between the different ways in which priests and lay people participate in the Church's mission, it is clear that the laity (both men and women) are not chattel, but rather have contributed much to the life of the Church through catechesis, service, witness, and evangelization (cf. LG 10–13). Methodius of Olympus (*De lepra,* 12 and 15) sings the praises of a Christian virgin who was literate

3.3 The apostles as forefathers of the People of God in the final age and representatives of the original relation of Christ to the Church

Characteristic of Jesus' public ministry is the fact that he enters into a relationship with the people to which he is sent. Jesus, the "Son of God" (cf. Heb 1:2), is the "*apostle* and *high priest* of our confession" (Heb 3:1; emphasis added). He derives his authority to proclaim salvation and to bring about the reign of God, not from his religious experiences or from the revolutionary dynamism of a reformer, but rather from his mission from the Father. He embodies the salvific will of God for all those men and women who become his disciples through conversion and faith (Mk 3:35).

The calling of the Twelve

Another significant feature of the prepaschal ministry of Jesus, though, is the fact that from the company of his disciples he *calls* a permanent group, the "Twelve", so as to let them *share in his mission*, in order that each of them might, in his person, *represent* him as one sent by God.

In a unique, majestic act he *calls* those whom he has *chosen*. He "*created*" them to be the Twelve—because they share in his mission they are also called "apostles" (Mk 6:30)—so that they might be *with him*, and form a *communio* with him. He then *sent them out* to preach faith and repentance *in his name*, to proclaim the gospel that the reign of God is near, and, with his authority (*exousia*), to accomplish his saving work in word and sign (Mk 3:13–19; 6:6–13). They are

---

and who worked with great success as a teacher in Lycia, probably as an official instructor of candidates for Baptism.

also the representatives of the twelve tribes of the covenant people, which in the final messianic age is reestablished so as to fulfill its task of being a sign and an instrument of salvation for all peoples. Thus they are the foundation stone of the Temple, i.e., of the eschatological People of God (cf. Mt 19:28; Eph 2:20, 3:5; Rev 21:12ff.). Because they share in Jesus' mission and actually represent him, he who hears their word hears the Word of Christ (Lk 10:16; 1 Thess 2:13).

On the basis of the Easter appearances, the Twelve (apostles) with Peter at their head guarantee that the prepaschal company of disciples is identical to the Church, which came into being through the Paschal Mystery and the Pentecostal outpouring of the Holy Spirit (Lk 24:34; Acts 1:21; 1 Cor 15:3–5; Gal 1:17f.). The words of ecclesiological commission are intended and are valid for them. As authorized witnesses they are sent out into the whole world to proclaim the gospel of the Cross and Resurrection, to make disciples of men, i.e., to lead them to the Church and to baptize them in the name of Jesus the Son, and of the Father, and of the Holy Spirit (Mt 28:19). To them is given the instruction to carry out, in word and symbolic action, the eucharistic memorial of the New Covenant (1 Cor 11:26; Lk 22:19). Just as Jesus did, the apostles (who preside over the Church) are to take bread and wine into their hands, pronounce the prayer of thanksgiving, and distribute the gifts to the faithful. By holding fast to the "apostles' teaching and fellowship [*koinonia*], to the breaking of bread and the prayers" (Acts 2:42), the Church is built up as the Body of Christ (1 Cor 10:16). The apostolate of Paul, which is based on a special vocation, is associated with that of the Twelve, without calling into question the fundamental importance of Peter and the Twelve in the Church.

Even though the term "apostle" as a set *title* for a particular *office* develops only gradually and is described somewhat differently in the writings of Luke and of Paul, they are not referring to completely different realities. They mean the twelve witnesses and emissaries (apostles) of Jesus, authorized by the risen Lord, to whom Paul is associated by reason of a special revelation and mission. Paul numbers among them also James, the brother of the Lord, and "all the apostles" to whom the risen Lord appeared (1 Cor 15:7). The early Christian missionaries who were particularly connected with the apostolate of Paul (Barnabas, Silvanus, Timothy, Titus, Epaphras, Epaphroditus, Apollos) have a share in his apostolic authority and power as his closest coworkers (delegates, disciples, and followers). Like Paul and with him, they are "cooperator[s] with God [*synergon tou Theou*] in the Gospel of Christ" (literal translation of 1 Thess 3:2), or they work "[as] a faithful minister of Christ on [his] behalf" (Col 1:7). As leading men (*hegoumenoi*, cf. Acts 15:22; Heb 13:7, 17, 24) of the Church (of Antioch) and presiders at their liturgies, they are also called apostles, prophets, and teachers (Acts 13:1; 14:3, 15:32; Lk 11:49; 1 Cor 12:28; Gal 6:6; Eph 4:11). They should be distinguished from the envoys sent by the congregations and from the Christians who collaborated in a general way with the Church's mission and offered the Apostle support in one instance or another (cf. Rom 16:7, which refers to Andronicus and Junia/Junias as "men of note among the apostles" or, in an alternative reading, "men who are esteemed by the apostles").[19]

Christ's presence in those whom he has sent

As appointed shepherds (Jn 21:16ff.), the apostles make present Christ the Good Shepherd, who laid down his life for his sheep (Jn 10:11). Precedence (*excellentia*) or "being the first" consists here in being the slave of all, just as "the Son of man also came not to be served but to serve, and to give his life as a ransom for many" (Mk 10:44–45). In proclaiming that Jesus Christ is Lord, the apostles are the servants of the faithful for Jesus' sake (cf. 2 Cor 4:5). To the

[19] Cf. Karl Kertelge, "Frauen im Neuen Testament: Dienste und Ämter", in Müller, *Frauen*.

apostles as the "ministers of the Word" (Lk 1:2; Acts 6:4) and "ministers of a new covenant" (2 Cor 3:6) is entrusted "the message of reconciliation. So we are ambassadors for Christ, God making his appeal through us" (2 Cor 5:19–20; cf. Tit 1:3). Upon the apostles is conferred the ministry of the new covenant, in the Spirit, not in a written code (2 Cor 3:6). They are fellow workers in building the house (*oikos*) of God (1 Cor 3:9; 2 Cor 6:1), which is the Temple of the Spirit, the People of God, and the Body of Christ. They are "servants of Christ" and thus "stewards (*oikonomoi*) of the mysteries of God" (1 Cor 4:1), that is, of his plan of salvation revealed in Christ. By virtue of the gift bestowed on him by God, the Apostle works as "a minister [Gk: *lei-tourgon*] of Christ Jesus to the Gentiles in the priestly service [Gk: *hierougounta*] of the gospel of God, so that the offering of the Gentiles may be acceptable, sanctified by the Holy Spirit" (Rom 15:16).

The Apostle, who proclaims the good news of reconciliation *in Christ's stead* and makes God's love present in his love for the Christian community, has betrothed the Church to one *Husband*, thereby leading the Church as a *pure virgin* to Christ (2 Cor 11:2). He is, as it were, the "friend of the bridegroom" (Jn 3:29; cf. Hos 2; Jer 2:1–7; 51:5; Is 49:14–21; 50:1, 54:1–10; 62:4f.; Ezek 16:8; Mt 22:2f.; Eph 5:25–33; Rev 19:7; 21:2).

For the faithful in the Church, the Apostle "became [their] father in Christ Jesus through the gospel" (1 Cor 4:15). He is gentle with them all, "like a nurse taking care of her children" (1 Thess 2:7; Gal 4:19), although as an apostle he could have made his authority felt. The Apostle represents the maternal love of Christ; like Yahweh (cf. Is 49:15), whom he called his Father, he wanted to gather Israel as a hen gathers and protects her chicks under her wings (cf. Mt 23:37; Lk 13:34).[20]

The apostolate of the Twelve and of Paul—the dynamic origin of the priestly ministry of teaching and shepherding

In historical continuity with the authority and organizational competence of the apostles, at the moment of transition to the postapostolic period, the foundation was laid for the ministerial office held by those who were placed over the churches: the ministry of the *episkopoi* and *presbyteroi*. They represent Christ as they perform fundamental services: the ministry of the Word, the celebration of sacramental liturgy, and the pastoral care of the Church. As Vatican II puts it:

> In the person of the bishops, then, to whom the priests render assistance, the Lord Jesus Christ, supreme high priest, is present in the midst of the faithful. Though seated at the right hand of God the Father, he is not absent from the assembly of his pontiffs; on the contrary indeed, it is above all through their signal service that he preaches the Word of God to all peoples and administers without cease to the faithful the sacraments of faith; that through their paternal care (cf. 1 Cor 4:15) he

[20] On the development of the biblical and patristic idea that the bishop mediates life in a higher sense through Baptism, the conferring of the Holy Spirit, and the Reconciliation of sinners, and thus becomes the spiritual father of the church, see especially Henri de Lubac, *"Väterlichkeit der amtlichen Diener"* [the paternal quality of those who serve in office] in the volume edited by the same author, *Quellen kirchlicher Einheit* [Sources of Church unity] (Einsiedeln, 1974), pp. 156–71. Pope Damasus I (*Ep. ad Gall. episc.* 2) compares the relation of the bishop to the Church with the indissoluble bond that unites the husband to his wife and family. Cf. Eusebius of Caesarea, *Dem. evang.* 1, 9, 14ff.; Epiphanius, *Haer.* 59, 4, 1–7; Ephrem, *Poem. Nisib.* 19; John Chrysostom, *Sac.* 3, 6; Augustine, *Serm. de ord. episc.* 7 (PLS 2, 642).

incorporates, by a supernatural rebirth, new members into his body. (LG 21)

Already in the local churches founded by Paul—for which the "apostle of Christ Jesus" (1 Cor 1:1), "[the one] called . . . [and] set apart for the gospel of God" (Rom 1:1), bears the overall responsibility and anxiety (2 Cor 11:28)—there is mention of those who are "placed over" the Christian community [Latin: *qui praesunt*] (1 Thess 5:12, cf. Rom 12:8); these men have "devoted themselves to the service of the saints", and Paul urges the faithful "to be subject to such men and to every fellow worker and laborer" (1 Cor 16:15). The *proistamenoi*—which was already in the Septuagint (LXX) a title for those set over others in the people of the Old Covenant—are probably identical with the *episkopoi* (Phil 1:1), who are assisted by helpers (*diakonoi*). Here, too, it is important, indeed, essential that the title of *episkopos* (as shepherd) is anticipated by the usage of the LXX. In the Greek translation of the Old Testament, which served as a standard for the New Testament writers, the title refers to God (Job 20:29, LXX Wis 1:6), the Messiah (Is 40:11; Jer 31:10), and the "shepherds of Israel".[21] As with the *proistamenoi* and *hegoumenoi* (Acts 15:22; Heb 13:7, 17, 24),[22] the term implies both standing up for those in one's care and also pastoral (i.e., nonpolitical) leadership and guidance (to good pastures). The "presiders" (*prokathemenoi*) in the Church are the presbyters, with the bishop at the head of the company of presbyters and deacons.[23]

[21] Hermann Wolfgang Beyer, article "ἐπίσκοπος", in ThWNT 2:595–619.

[22] Cf. Bo Reicke, article "προΐστημι", in ThWNT 6:700–703.

[23] Ignatius of Antioch, *Magn.* 6; Pastor Hermae, *Visio* 2, 2, 6; 3, 9, 7; *Sim.* 31, 5f.

The presbyters, too (literally: those who are "advanced"[24] in age or, here, in rank), may be described elsewhere as leaders of the churches (1 Tim 5:17; cf. Justin, 1 *Apol.* 65).[25] The leaders of the twenty-four priestly classes in the Old Testament already were called "presbyters" (1 Chron 24:2–19; Josephus Flavius, Ant. 7, 365–68). "The apostles and presbyters [elders, RSVC]" (Acts 15:4, 6, 22) appear as the supreme authority of the church of Jerusalem, under the direction of Peter and later of James (Acts 21:18), "the brother of the Lord". Associated with them are the teachers, prophets, and apostles (Acts 13:1; 14:3; cf. Lk 11:49) of the church of Antioch.

This continuity with the apostles is particularly emphasized, and its ecclesiological relevance is demonstrated by the report that the apostles Barnabas and Paul (Acts 14:14) "ordained to them priests in every church" (Acts 14:13, Douay-Rheims). It is self-evident that in his farewell speech in Miletus the Apostle, anticipating the time after his death, entrusts the presbyters to God and to the Word of his grace, through which the Church is built up as the communion of

[24] The translation of the term *presbyteros* as "elder" in the German Church Unity translation of the Bible [*Einheitsübersetzung*; also in the RSVC, cf. 1 Pet 5] lacks depth of expression, since the expression "elder" is not used at all in German for an official position (unless for a *Rats-kollegium*, a board of advisors). A meaningful translation would have to be based instead on *Vor-steher* ["pre-fect", one placed before or ahead of others]. The New Testament understands a presbyter to be someone appointed by the apostles to proclaim the gospel and to shepherd the church; therefore the expression would have to be translated as "priest" to convey the meaning. In fact the German word *Priester* [and the English word "priest"] come from *presbyter*, via the Frankish and French words *prestre* and *prêtre*.

[25] Cf. Günter Bornkamm, article "πρέσβυς κτλ", in ThWNT 6:651–83.

saints. For the presbyters are appointed by the Holy Spirit to be bishops [*episkopos* = overseers, or "guardians" RSVC], so as to give a shepherd's care to the Church, God's flock (Acts 20:28; Ezek 34:11–16; Jer 3:15).

In the pastoral letters the Apostle's disciples, Timothy and Titus, provide the continuity between the ministry of those placed at the head of the churches and Paul, the "preacher and apostle and teacher" of the Gentiles (2 Tim 1:11; 1 Tim 2:7). They are authorized by the Apostle through the conferral of "Spirit and power" in the sign of the laying on of hands (2 Tim 1:6), and thus they are ordained to the presbyterate (1 Tim 4:14); the Apostle's disciples, in turn, are responsible for appointing *presbyteroi* and *episkopoi* by the imposition of hands and prayer (1 Tim 5:22; Tit 1:5), and in certain cases they are assigned to supervise them (1 Tim 5:19). Their task is essentially to expound the Word of God in instruction and proclamation[26] and to care for God's Church as men set over her, since the Church is the "people and house" of God (1 Tim 3:1–7, 15; 5:17; Tit 1:5–9; 1 Pet 2:5, 9; 5:1–4; cf. Jas 5:14). They are divinely empowered and also in continuity with the commissioning authority of the apostles. How are we to understand the concurrence of these two factors? The answer is evident in the New Testament sources just mentioned, which are from the time immediately after the lives of the apostles ended. During this period of transition

---

[26] It is therefore incorrect to interpret the pastoral letters, as is often done, as though they documented a move away from the original teaching "charism" and its institutionalization as an office. Just as the charism of prophetic speech and teaching is within the province of every Christian (women have been officially recognized by the Church as teachers), apostolic teaching—that is, the authority to proclaim the gospel —remains the mission entrusted specifically to those who are called to be apostles and bishops or presbyters.

it is not a question of a Church with pneumatic-charismatic foundations being replaced by one that is spiritless and legalistic; what emerges, rather, is the sacramental character of the Church, which includes the ministry of the bishops and presbyters. In the rite of laying on of hands, the conferral of spiritual authority and the vocation to a way of life that prolongs Christ's pastoral ministry is symbolized and at the same time effected. The anachronistic hermeneutic mentioned a moment ago, with its purely sociological perspective, inevitably leads to serious misunderstandings also with regard to the Catholic distinction between "priests and laity" within the Church.

When representatives of the liberal "theology of cultural Christianity" (Rudolf Sohm, Adolf von Harnack) interpreted the transition from the apostolic to the postapostolic Church as a decline from an originally prophetic community of heart and mind, devoid of offices, to a legalistic, authoritarian institution with fixed dogmas, in which a priestly caste ruled over the laity (*Frühkatholizismus*, "early Catholicism"), their diagnosis of early Church history was not based on objective reality but on false presuppositions (derived from Max Weber) about the meaning of "charismatic". By taking this term—anachronistically and inappropriately—in the *sociological* instead of the *theological* sense, they managed to understand it as being in opposition to "institutional". The Pauline communities, nevertheless, owed their existence originally to Christ's Word, which was promulgated by the Apostle's authority and which continuously shapes the Church. It is not that the Apostle founded the churches and then left their final formation to the workings of the Spirit (misunderstood in a transcendental way), which subsequently produced churches in the sense of communities organized along congregational lines. Rather, it is the Spirit who, *by means of* the apostolic proclamation, gives rise to the Church and who guides the minds of all members of the Church in such a way that the various gifts of grace, ministries, and missions, as well as the offices of presiders, apostles, prophets, and teachers, serve to *build up the Church* (1 Cor 14:26f.; Eph 4:11). Charisms could hardly have been understood as entitlements allowing individuals to segregate themselves from the community or competitively to claim a position of advantage. "Office" and "Spirit" are by no means opposites. Indeed, Moses, the mediator of the Old Covenant, had appointed seventy rulers (presbyters) precisely by putting upon them something of his spirit (Num 11:25). In the Church, all are members of the Body of Christ, but not everyone is an apostle, a prophet, or a teacher. No one can lay claim to these commissions simply because he feels called by the Spirit, because they are instituted by God (1 Cor 12:28).

The continuity with the apostles comes to the fore when Peter describes himself as a "fellow presbyter" and clearly expounds the way in which the presbyters represent Christ. They are to shepherd God's flock, *watching over* them [*episkopountes*] (1 Pet 5:2). They are "examples to the flock" (v. 3), whose real shepherd is Christ, "the Shepherd and Guardian [*episkopos*] of your souls" (1 Pet 2:25; Mt 26:31; Heb 13:20). The Church Fathers[27] refer to this when they explain the special way in which the priest represents Christ (Head/ Shepherd/Bridegroom of the Body/flock/Bride)[28] and speak of the priest as the "icon of Christ".[29]

---

[27] A comprehensive collection of the most important patristic passages on the priesthood can be found in: Florián Rodero, *El Sacerdocio en los Padres de la Iglesia* (Madrid, 1993).

[28] On the subject of "begetting spiritually, not bodily" and "spiritual fatherhood through the proclamation of the Word", see Origen, *Hom. in Lev.* 4:6; *hom. in Gen.* 5:6; *hom. in Num.* 20:2. See also Stefan Heid, *Celibacy in the Early Church* (San Francisco: Ignatius Press, 2001), pp. 119–20. Chrysostom expresses the same idea in *Sac.* 3, 6: To the priest are entrusted "spiritual travails" or birth-pangs (cf. Gal 4:19), and he has the responsibility of "guarding the Bride of Christ".

[29] Theodore of Mopsuestia, *Hom.* 15, 24 (FC 17/2, P. Bruns, pp. 407– 9): "Therefore through the priest we picture in our minds, as though in a kind of portrait (εἰκών), Christ our Lord, whom we view as the One who redeemed and saved us by his self-sacrifice. Through the deacons

There is in fact a distinction between the membership in the Church which is common to all by virtue of Baptism, together with full collaboration in the collective mission, on the one hand, and the particular apostolic, priestly duties of the bishops, presbyters, and deacons (1 Clement 40:5), on the other. This distinction, furthermore, has its foundations already in the New Testament. Of course, it is not a question of a gradual differentiation and valuation of what it means to be a Christian; the distinction is—as the Second Vatican Council emphasizes—precisely an *essential* one, a distinction

---

(διάκονοι), however, who perform their service at the Re-enactment, we impress upon our understanding the invisible, ministering spirits (cf. Heb 1:14), who have taken their place in that ineffable service. They are the ones who bring forward this Victim and the symbols (τύποι) of this Victim, arrange them, and place them on the awe-inspiring table." [Translated from the German.]

Ambrose, *De Obitu Valentiniani* 79b (CSEL 73, 367): "Sed tu in sacerdote dominum requirebas" [But you sought for the Lord in the priest]. Roger Gryson (*Le prêtre selon saint Ambroise* [Louvain, 1968], p. 329) summarizes the theology of the priesthood in Ambrose's writings as follows: "*Bref, le Prêtre visible est l'image du grand-prêtre invisible. Non pas une 'ombre' vide, menteuse même, comme les prêtres selon l'ordre d'Aaron, mais une 'image' qui porte en elle la réalité qu'elle représente. . . . À travers un homme, choisi et consacré pour cette fonction, c'est le Christ-prêtre qui se révèle et qui agit*" [In short, the visible Priest is the image of the invisible high priest. Not an empty 'shadow' like the priests of the Aaronic order, but an 'image' that contains the reality that it represents. . . . Through a man, chosen and consecrated for this purpose, it is Christ the Priest who reveals himself and acts"].

On the subject of how the priest represents Christ in preaching and in his eucharistic ministry, cf. Felix Genn, *Trinität und Amt nach Augustinus* (Einsiedeln, 1985), pp. 201–9, 236–42; Aimé Georges Martimort, "Der Wert der theologischen Formel 'In der Person Christi' ", in Gerhard Ludwig Müller, ed., *Der Empfänger des Weihesakraments: Quellen zur Lehre und Praxis der Kirche, nur Männern das Weihesakrament zu spenden* (Würzburg, 1999), pp. 423–32.

not in modes of being Christian, but rather in being called to a specific ministry (LG 10). It results from the fact that certain believers are entrusted with the apostolic ministry of proclaiming the Word and administering Baptism, of pronouncing the eucharistic words that commemorate Christ's offering of his life and make present his sacrifice, and also of anointing the sick (Jas 5:14), forgiving sins (Mt 18:18; Jn 20:23), and exercising the pastoral ministry of Christ; for they carry out their duties as a "type" of Christ (1 Pet 5:2–3), and in his stead they call people to reconciliation (2 Cor 5:19f.).

"Priests" and "laity"

In the juxtaposition of the bishops and priests (who are appointed to serve as shepherds) with the faithful, the absolute priority of Christ the Good Shepherd as the foundation of the Church is manifested in a sacramental way, as well as the juxtaposition of Head and members in the Body of Christ, which is the Church (cf. "[A]part from me you can do nothing" [Jn 15:5] and the significance of this saying for salvation, both objective and subjective). Therefore, in a fundamental way, the "layman", too, is not defined negatively by his exclusion from priestly functions in the apostolic ministry of reconciliation (2 Cor 5:20; Tit 1:5); rather, he is defined positively by his sanctification, through Baptism, and thus by his full membership in the Church and his participation in the priestly-kingly-prophetic mission of the Church as a whole (1 Pet 2:5, 9; 4:10; Rev 1:6; Ex 19:6). The "layman" (1 Clement 40:5) is not a passive member of the Church, as distinguished from the priest, characterized by "what he cannot do". The layman is defined positively by belonging to the People of God and thus by collaborating in the universal mission of the Church in *martyria*, *leiturgia*, and *diakonia*. The ministry of "shepherds and teachers", following that of the "apostles, . . . prophets, . . . [and] evangelists" (Eph 4:11; 2:20; 3:5), on the other hand, does not mean a privileged position for a "caste" separated from the community of believers. An essential distinction between ordinary Christians and the perfect ("*electi*") was found in the Gnostic groups, whereas in the Catholic Church the priests are distinguished from the faithful in general by their God-given office (*oikonomia*), through which they serve the entire Church (cf. Col 1:25; Eph 3:2).[30] God himself gives priests to the Church "for the equipment of the saints, for the work of ministry, for building up the body of Christ" (Eph 4:12).

Apostolic *authority* with respect to teaching and liturgy does not degenerate into a means of wielding power over others and of promoting self-interest as long as it is upheld by the self-giving *love* of the apostle, who takes as his ex-

---

[30] Cf. Klauck, *Religiöse Umwelt*, pp. 184ff. With the pronounced separation of the ecclesiastical states of clerics, monks, and laity from the fourth century on, there is a clear awareness that the laity are Church in the full sense. Men and women are involved in catechesis, the selection of bishops, administering Baptism in emergencies, charitable works. This period, especially in the region of Syria, saw the beginnings of the office of deaconesses, who instructed women and performed charitable and pastoral services for them. Cf. Hubert Jedin, ed., "Die Reichskirche nach Konstantin dem Grossen", in HKG 2/1 (Freiburg/Basel/Vienna, 1973), p. 345. The disciplinary ruling (e.g., of the Synod of Laodicea in 393) that women should not enter the sanctuary applies both to them and to lay men. It is a question here of the distinction between clerics and laity in the liturgy, and not of some privilege of men or an exclusion of women from the realm of the sacred. John Chrysostom (*Sac.* 2, 2) explains that the distinction between priests and laity cannot be equated with the distinction between men and women, saying that in the appointing of priests as leaders and shepherds, "the female sex must retire before the magnitude of the task, and the majority of men also."

ample the dedication of Christ, the Chief Shepherd of the
Church (cf. 2 Cor 5:14f.; 10:8f.; 11:2; Jn 15:9–16; 21:5;
1 Pet 5:1–4).

3.4 *In what sense are bishops and presbyters "priests"?*

If becoming a Christian takes place in the power of the
Spirit, this is still expressed in the rite of Baptism. Similarly,
conferring the power to proclaim the Word effectively in
the Spirit, and to pasture God's flock, took place through a
rite in which the apostle authorized the leaders and teachers
—a rite incorporating Old Testament elements, such as the
laying on of hands and the *epiklesis* of the Holy Spirit (Acts
14:23; 20:28). Since faith arises through the proclamation
of the Word, and only someone sent by Christ is authorized
to exercise this ministry (Rom 10:14–17; 2 Cor 5:18f.), the
"shepherds/pastors and teachers" must already have received
spiritual authority, in historical continuity with the apostles,
precisely in the rite of conferring ministries (1 Tim 4:14;
2 Tim 1:6; Tit 1:5). The notion of an exclusively vertical
descent of the Holy Spirit contradicts the historical continuity and the visible mediation that are part of the conferring
of Orders, just as they are in Baptism and the Eucharist.

  We are dealing with a deeply rooted, tenacious misunder-
standing, when people consider merely the externals of the
Church from the perspective of the history of religion or
sociology and maintain that in her earliest days the Church
had no priests, but only "community officials" who were
responsible for routine organizational matters in the life
of the congregation. According to this view, the spiritual
proceedings—such as the administration of Baptism, "the
thanksgiving and breaking of bread", and the authoritative,
apostolic proclamation of doctrine—had been entrusted to

those who, ad hoc, knew that they were charismatic, spontaneously impelled by the working of the Spirit descending from on high. This way of viewing it is usually justified by referring to the fact that the responsible parties in the Christian communities were described using profane titles like "overseer" or "elder", which is said to indicate unmistakably that they were essentially different from the heathen cultic priests. In actuality, a division of the cosmos into a sacred realm and a profane one is foreign to the religion of the Bible. It is true that the heathens remarked the lack of any cult of the gods, any temple or cultic sacrifices among the Christians.[31] Phenotypically, the Christian priesthood had nothing whatsoever to do with pagan cultic worship, and the Eucharist, which makes Christ's sacrifice of himself truly present in a symbolic ritual through the Word, is entirely different from the pagan sacrifices.[32]

[31] Cf. Theophilus, *Autol.* 3, 29; Minucius Felix, *Octavius* 8.

[32] "Many proponents of the latter position understand the development to be by and large the result of social pressure on the Church, since religions in antiquity had a priesthood. But this explanation seems unsatisfactory. At the time when the priestly terminology first appeared, the Christian apologists still insisted that Christianity was not just a religion like any other. Furthermore Judaism, which compensated for the loss of the Temple by recognizing the synagogue worship service as a substitute for the Temple cult, managed to do without [conforming to pagan patterns]" (Paul Frederick Bradshaw, article "Priester/Priestertum, III/1, Christliches Priesteramt: Geschichtlich", in TRE 27 [1997]: 414–21, 416f.). If the claim that Christianity adopted pagan notions of priesthood were correct, then the institution of Roman priestesses would necessarily have been adopted as well. Cf. Klauck, *Religiöse Umwelt*, p. 66: "The office of high priest in the imperial cult was also open to women —not, as was first supposed, in their capacity as the wives of male high priests, but entirely in their own right." There is no evident reason why the Church should have allowed the office of the bishop and the presbyter to be thoroughly transformed to resemble the office of the male *pontifex maximus* but not the office of the female counterpart. In reality sacramental Orders historically and objectively have nothing to do

If, nevertheless, the bishop and the presbyter are called "priests" (*hiereus, sacerdos*) in isolated instances in the first century and then more and more frequently from the second and third centuries on, then this does not mean that a fateful lapse into Jewish or even pagan ways of thought was under way.[33] No substantial transformation of community functionaries into cultic priests took place (by which the priesthood supposedly "attained ontological status"), bringing with it the duties of offering sacrifices for the *salus publica* and of divining the will of the gods through the inspection of entrails, oracles, etc.

The point of reference for the development of Christian terminology is, rather, in the thoroughly theological concept of the symbolic (typological) representation of Christ, the Priest and Shepherd, who gave up his life.[34] *He* acts in the person of the bishop and the presbyter. Just as the apostles are termed "ministers of the Word" (Lk 1:2; Acts 6:4), so

---

with the pagan cultic priesthood, and the connection between Orders and male recipients has nothing to do with the religious and cultural features of the social milieu. Cf. the description of the character and duties of the priests of the Roman imperial cult, which are in no way comparable with the ministries of bishops and priests, in Basil Studer, *Schola christiana: Die Theologie zwischen Nizäa und Chalzedon* (Paderborn, 1998), p. 71.

[33] Compare this to the dated but still illuminating discussions of Karl Prümm, *Christentum als Neuheitserlebnis: Durchblick durch die christlich-antike Begegnung* (Freiburg, 1939), pp. 311–31.

[34] Ignatius of Antioch, *Magnesians* 6; Cyprian, *Epist.* 60[63], 14: "For if Jesus Christ, our Lord and God, is himself the chief priest of God the Father, and has first offered himself a sacrifice to the Father, and has commanded this to be done in commemoration of himself, certainly that priest truly discharges the office of Christ, who imitates that which Christ did; and he then offers a true and full sacrifice in the Church to God the Father, when he proceeds to offer it according to what he sees Christ himself to have offered."

too the "elders . . . who labor in preaching and teaching" (1 Tim 5:17, "*presbyteri . . . qui laborant in verbo et doctrina*") are above all else *priests of the Word*[35] because of their duty and authority to evangelize, lead, and edify the Church with "the apostles' teaching" (Acts 2:42; 2 Tim 1:14). The Word includes apostolic preaching and also its sacramental incarnation in the sacraments. The proclamation of the Word and the liturgy take place through the shepherd of the congregation, who in their regard portrays Christ's self-giving, through which the Church continually becomes "one flesh" with her Head and Bridegroom.

In this connection one can speak of a transformation of the presbyter into a sort of pagan cultic priest in Christian robes only if one misunderstands the Sacrifice of the Mass, mistaking its sacramental character for something pagan and cultic, thus narrowing down apostolic ministry—which includes the ministry of the word and the pastoral ministry of building up the Church—and restricting its priestly character to the authority to consecrate (which is furthermore misinterpreted in a magical sense).[36]

---

[35] Cf. John Chrysostom, who in his homily on the day of his ordination to the priesthood says, "Let his sacrifice be the Word" (*Homilia cum presbyter ordinatus fuit*, PG 48: 694, 699). In a Byzantine prayer of priestly ordination we find the expression "to perform the sacred office of the Word" (Jean Morin, *Commentarius de sacris Ecclesiae ordinationibus*, 2d ed. [Antwerp, 1695], p. 22; references in Bradshaw's article, "Priester/Priestertum, III/1", in TRE 27:417). Cf. also Peterson, *Brief an die Römer,* who on pages 18ff. points out the intrinsic unity, typical in Paul's writings, of gospel, apostolic ministry, apostolic-priestly Eucharist, and liturgy. Cf. Eugenio Romero Pose, "Apuntes sobre el ministerio en San Ireneo (La sencillez de Dios y del hombre)", EstTrin 32 (1997): 1–42; cf. also John Chrysostom, *Sac.* 4, 4, etc.

[36] Drawing upon a most extensive range of source material, Manuel Guerra Gómez, *El sacerdocio femenino (en las religiones greco-romanas y en el cristianismo de los primeros siglos)* (Toledo, 1987), shows that "priestesses"

The supposition that in early New Testament times prophetesses, too, or any member at all of the congregation could pronounce the words of the eucharistic epiclesis[37] has no historical basis whatsoever. The Lord's Supper or the "breaking of the bread" stands side by side with the teaching of the apostles; as part of tradition, it is the memorial, celebrated, and actualized in the Word, of the sacrifice of Christ's Body, which through this ceremony effects the *communio* of the Church. This being so, then the Eucharistic Prayer is a part, or, better yet, the culmination of the word of reconciliation that is entrusted to the apostles. The only time in the New Testament that the presider at the Eucharist is mentioned expressly, it is the Apostle Paul, who on the first day of the week explains the Word for the assembly *and* breaks bread (Acts 20:7, 11). For the Christian liturgy, in contrast to the pagan cult, the intrinsic unity of Gospel

---

are often encountered in pagan cults, but at the same time that the Christian priesthood, because of its apostolic origins and its orientation toward proclamation and pastoral care, has an entirely different character from that of the pagan cultic ministry and therefore cannot be grouped together with the latter in the same category.

[37] Cf. Heiler, *Frau*, p. 105. "Now, since prophetic women had the right to pray freely, we must assume that they also pronounced the great prayer of thanksgiving, through which bread and wine were consecrated and became the sacramental food. For the Church at large, it is true, there are no records testifying explicitly to this practice, but there certainly is for the 'heretical' congregations, both Gnostic and Montanist. Since these sects continued to hold fast to the forms of the early Church, even after the Church at large had outgrown them or had deliberately rejected them, we must conclude that female prophets, too, pronounced the Eucharistic Prayers and thus blessed the bread and wine or, to use our language: consecrated." What an astonishing methodology: in the absence of explicit testimony to draw a certain conclusion, groping along a chain of at least three mere conjectures to draw inferences about unknown terrain.

proclamation and Eucharist is an essential characteristic of Christ's victory and of *communio* with Christ.[38]

Closely related to the apostolic ministry are the prophets and teachers (Acts 13:1), whereby it is a question of ministries instituted by God (1 Cor 12:28; cf. 1 Jn 4:1f.) and not of the charism of prophetic speech. These "apostles, prophets, and teachers" are those who proclaim the gospel, who pronounce the "Eucharistic Prayer" in the assemblies (*Didache* 10:7), which is also the duty of the bishops (*Didache* 15:1), whom the deacons assist. If the proclamation of the Word and saying the Eucharistic Prayer were not essentially connected with the ministries of the bishop and of the priest from the start, then the question would necessarily arise, what factors prompted such a development to take place, so that in the "Catholic Church" only that Eucharist is recognized which is celebrated with the bishop or a presbyter appointed by him presiding, as Ignatius already testifies (*Smyrn.* 8, 1f.) at the beginning of the second century.[39]

In the celebration of the Eucharist, bread and wine are brought to the presider of the church, so that he says over the gifts the *prayer of thanksgiving* directed to the Father through the Son and the Holy Spirit.[40]

[38] Cf. Peterson, *Brief an die Römer*, p. 20.

[39] In doing so he is obviously only recalling a universally accepted concept, since there is not the slightest trace of any irritation or controversy that might have resulted. Citing Pierre-Thomas Camelot (SCh 10, 46), Henri de Lubac points this out in "The *Dialogue on the Priesthood* by Saint John Chrysostom", in *Theology in History,* trans. Anne Englund Nash (San Francisco: Ignatius Press, 1996), pp. 23–33, at p. 30.

[40] Justin, 1 *Apol.* 65.

3.5 *In the early Church, who could receive Holy Orders validly?*

Even though there is no doubt about the common vocation of all men and women to salvation and to full membership in the Church, it is still obvious at first glance that the apostolic ministry of the Twelve and the apostolate of Paul, of James the brother of the Lord, and of other "prophets and teachers" (Acts 13:1) was in fact carried out by men only. Furthermore already in New Testament times there are initial reflections about the fact that only men have exercised the apostolic ministry (in the strict sense) and the offices (*tagma*, Gk., *ordo*, Lat.) of bishop, presbyter, and deacon that arose from it.[41] The work of women in and for the Church does

[41] Women in the Church, like all believers, are called to participate in the universal mission and the common life of the Church as priestly-kingly-prophetic People of God (1 Pet 2:5, 9; 1 Cor 11:5). Occasionally they also perform specific services or tasks on an ongoing basis (Rom 16:1–4; 1 Tim 5:9). It is not possible to speak of an exclusion of women from equal participation in the Church's diaconate, apostolate, and mission during the period of the later New Testament writings (from A.D. 60 to about 100), due to the pressure of Old Testament and Roman concepts of law, through a conscious or unconscious conformity to the subordinate role of women in the religious practices of antiquity, and to the structure of the male-dominated *oikos* [household] (Rosemarie Nürnberg, "Todestag von Edith Stein", in Rudolf Englert, ed., *Woran sie glaubten—Wofür sie lebten* [Munich, 1993], p. 229). For this interpretation suggests itself only if one limits the exercise of ecclesial mission to the clergy, or considers the continuance of the lay apostolate as something possible only through conferral of the Sacrament of Holy Orders. Women have never held the office of bishop or presbyter, which proceeded from the apostolic ministry, and yet they played an essential and formative role in the intellectual and spiritual life of the Church inasmuch as they participated in the common apostolate and universal priesthood of the Church. It is striking that the early Church, in dogmatic and ethical essentials (the unicity and indissolubility of marriage, the prohibition against infanticide, the imperial cult and participation in the pagan rites with their "lying myths", which in the view of the

not depend on the office of bishop or presbyter. Indeed, the pagans were struck by the fact that women had equal dignity as human beings among the Christians, because of their full participation in the life of the Church. Women appeared as leading personages (in spiritual and intellectual matters) in ecclesial life and in *ecclesial* offices. In the rise of Christianity and its societal power, women played an essential part.[42] Women also were prominent in *ecclesial* offices, especially in the area of *diakonia*, which is a fundamental and essential activity of the Church (enrolled widow, deaconess, religious superior). These ecclesial offices and services, nevertheless, are distinct from the apostolic ministry of the "apostles, . . . prophets, . . . pastors and teachers" (Eph 4:11), the presiders, presbyters, and bishops. Besides, the social structures of the *oikos* of antiquity were not carried over into the Church, since managing a household well is only a qualification for a position of leadership in the Church, which represents the "house" of God, namely, God's people and temple. As to its scope, an ecclesial office is characterized by the ministry of the Word and by a share in Jesus' pastoral care for his flock, the Church, the house and people of God.

The fact that the apostolic mission remains the specific province of men called to this ministry is evident in the

---

Church Fathers were diabolical), set herself apart so radically from the Roman legal concepts and the mentality of contemporary society, and yet, on the other hand, that the pagan cultic priesthood is supposed to have been the model for the development of the offices of bishops and presbyters, who make Jesus Christ present in the midst of his flock, the Good Shepherd who laid down his life for his sheep (cf. John Chrysostom, *Sac.* 3, 6).

[42] Cf. Rodney Stark, *The Rise of Christianity: A Sociologist Reconsiders History* (Princeton: Princeton University Press, 1996), pp. 95–128. Cf. also the nuanced distinctions and analysis of Edith Ennen, *Frauen im Mittelalter*, 3d ed. (Munich, 1987).

method by which the full number of the Twelve was restored, as well as in the later handing on of apostolic authority. In order to replace Judas, *two men* are put forward, who were witnesses of Christ's public ministry and Resurrection, and Matthias is selected to receive a share (*cleros*) in the *diakonia* (ministry of the Word) and *episkope* (pastoral ministry of leadership) of the apostles (Acts 1:15–26).

Luke, who gives great emphasis to the collaboration of women in the early Church, reports that at the institution of the diaconate (the ministry of those who were appointed "to serve tables"), *seven men* were presented to the apostles (Acts 6:3) for the imposition of hands and that they later worked as evangelizers as well. The "prophets, teachers, and apostles" of the Church of Antioch are *men* (Acts 13:1–3, 15:22; cf. 1 Cor 12:28), as are the presbyters of the Church of Miletus (Acts 20:30). Any one who aspires to the office of bishop should be a *man* above reproach, who—after having proved himself as a good husband and father—will be a steward of the Church of the living God (1 Tim 3:2–3; Tit 1:7). The presbyter-episkopos must be a *man* (Tit 1:6) who holds "firm to the sure word as taught, so that he may be able to give instruction in sound doctrine and also to confute those who contradict it" (Tit 1:9).

Writings from the period immediately after the apostolic age, around the turn of the second century, assume that the ministry of the bishops, presbyters, and deacons is entrusted to men. The congregation is supposed to appoint *men*, who as bishops and deacons (*Didache* 15, 1) perform the services of the "apostles, prophets, and teachers" (*Didache* 11, 4; 15) and are their "high priests" (*Didache* 13, 3).

In the context of an early reflection on the apostolic basis for the episcopal ministry, the Roman Church reminds the Church at Corinth that the apostles gave orders that *proven men* should succeed them in the episcopal ministry and then hand this ministry on to *other proven men* (1 Clement 44, 2f.).

In the oldest Church constitution that has been handed down, it is specifically emphasized that, as distinguished from the sacramental imposition of hands that the bishop, presbyter, and deacon receive for the sake of the liturgical ministry, the enrollment of a woman in the widowed state is not carried out by means of a sacramental consecration.[43]

In all of the literary evidence of the subsequent centuries there is no question whatsoever about it: only a man *can* be appointed and ordained a bishop, a priest, or a deacon.

The question now, at any rate, is whether this practice contains a belief that touches upon the substance of the Sacrament of Holy Orders, or whether we are merely dealing with a *modus operandi* based on circumstances, disciplinary concerns, or custom, just as many public and religious offices in society were held only by men, without necessarily implying that there was an intrinsic connection with the male sex of the officeholder. Did the Church reflect on her practice and see it prescribed in Christ's institutional will? Did the Church on occasion defend this practice against contrary opinions and reason that it follows from the essence of the apostolic-priestly ministry?

3.6 The theological relevance of the Church's practice of conferring Holy Orders only on baptized males

In our search for the belief implied by the practice, we must make a fundamental distinction between fidelity to the institutional will of Jesus, who alone establishes the essence of

---

[43] Hippolytus, *Apostolic Tradition* 10.

the sacrament, and the secondary theological consideration of the reasons that may have caused Jesus to institute the sacrament in such a way that the person of the recipient is also a significant element.

A note on the style of argumentation

It is possible that, in the course of the history of theology, certain suitability arguments have been stated that are materially and objectively no longer convincing, among them possibly even *argumenta ad hominem* or arguments that derived their plausibility solely from customary practice, to which there seemed to be no alternative. This does not rule out the possibility that, in the course of our discussion, the intrinsic reason could emerge more clearly and the actual logic of the matter could become more intelligible.

This was the case, for example, in the area of eucharistic doctrine. The Real Presence of Christ in the eucharistic gifts always belonged to the Church's deposit of faith and was never in doubt. The theological form in which this truth was presented at any given time, however, may have been more or less illuminating and convincing. The *real reason* for the Eucharistic Presence is the will of Jesus and the working of the Spirit, which of course can be grasped only in faith, whereas the *explanatory reason* of theology is useful only to the extent that it is an elaboration of the real reason itself.

The most important conveyors of Sacred Tradition (Scripture, the Doctors of the Church, the Magisterium) must be interrogated as to their stance on the recipient of the Sacrament of Holy Orders. Do they simply intend to hand on the Church's deposit of faith? Or are they trying, by means of more or less plausible arguments of suitability, to explain more clearly why the Church regards her practice as an apostolic tradition, and thus as an expression of her faith that can

be traced back to Jesus' institutional will? Naturally, every articulation of the Church's faith comes about in an intellectual
and cultural climate conditioned by the times, upon which
certain thought patterns and clichéd notions (especially with
regard to man and woman) always leave their mark.

The fundamentally conditional quality of every human reflection upon the Word of God in the words of men is a
hermeneutic characteristic of present-day theology as well,
which is so concerned about an intrinsic distinction between
that which is binding in faith and its historically contingent
form of articulation. The fact that the Church Fathers occasionally make use of the thought patterns common in their
day in treating the question of the recipient of the Sacrament
of Orders does not in and of itself imply that their conviction
that the sacramental practice of the Church is rooted in Jesus'
institutional will is not after all an objective expression of a
revealed truth that is part of the Church's faith.

Finite reason is situated in history; it follows that man, in
the act of his intellect, always moves about in an inner tension between [1] an a priori transcendence directed toward
the intended reality and [2] the categorical representation of
that reality within the framework of language and, generally,
within a social and cultural milieu. Man upon reflection *can*
distinguish between the unconditional and the conditional
moments of his intellectual act; it is this fact *alone*, however,
that proves the existence of the two fundamental and recip-
rocally constitutive acts of the intellect. In contrast, in the
natural act of cognition, the faculty of reason is informed by
the reality that presents itself to be known, and this information affords the basis for the real knowledge. How much
more so, then, in matters of faith, is reason informed by the
God who presents himself to be known in his Word which

addresses man, all of which serves as the foundation for the fact of revelation and for the content of the knowledge imparted thereby.

The understanding of the faith that comes about historically, and which is firmly anchored in Sacred Scripture and in the binding faith tradition of the Church, is capable of determining the theological relevance of the *praxis Ecclesiae* through a process of understanding and in a decision rendered by the divinely authorized Magisterium of the bishops, as "successors to the apostles".[44]

It is a dogma of the Church that by its very nature the *one* apostolic ministry, which is structured both in the *communio* of the many ministers and also in its *unity, originating in Christ* (see Mk 3:13–19), is carried out in the sacramental unity of *one Ordo* of bishop, presbyter, and deacon. The Council of Trent says in its decree on Holy Orders [session 23, *Decretum de sacramento ordinis*], "Nemo dubitare debet, ordinem esse vere et proprie *unum* ex septem sanctae Ecclesiae sacramentis" [No one may doubt that Holy Orders is truly and properly *one* of the seven sacraments of Holy Church.] (DH 1766; cf. LG 20). If the office of bishop really (and not only nominally) has proved to be the principle of christologically based mission and of historical unity with the apostles, and if the multiplicity of presbyters (and of deacons), who represent the *communio* of the apostles, is ordered to the bishop and the presbyterium, then this can be understood historically and theologically only as the result of a dynamic that is inherent in and essential to the apostolic foundation of the Church, a dynamic that leads to the development of the Church and to service for the building up of the Church. And so the Church in fact did complete this process of differentiation unanimously, in her understanding of the faith, and in a remarkably short time, receiving it dogmatically as an authentic expression of God's will for his Church and for the *Ordo* of sacramental ministries permanently instituted on her behalf. Unequivocal evidence for this is found in the pastoral letters as well as in the letters of Ignatius of Antioch. In light of this, questions about the dogmatic distinction between the episcopacy and the presbyterate

[44] Irenaeus of Lyons, *Adversus haereses* 3, 3.

and about the exact boundaries between the sacramental diaconate and the *ordines minores*, while interesting for the history of theology, do not affect the dogmatic principle of the unity of Holy Orders; rather, they again presuppose this very unity and testify to it.[45]

An example of the more recent tendency to attribute the subdivision of the one Sacrament of Orders exclusively to the Church's freedom of development is the dissertation of Guido Bausenhart, *Das Amt in der Kirche. Eine not-wendende Neubestimmung* [Office in the Church: A new appraisal addressing needs] (Freiburg, 1999). The author is dealing with a nonbiblical category, "office", under which he subsumes the degrees of sacramental Orders and also the ecclesial offices to which laymen, too, can be appointed so as to collaborate with the hierarchy. Out of the ministry of leadership of the shepherds, which becomes evident in the New Testament, and a subordinate helping ministry of the deacons is distilled the mental construct, "office", and subsequently from this abstract notion the concrete ministries are deduced. The New Testament shows, on the contrary, that it was always concrete persons who are called and who hand on the mission. It is never a hypostatized conceptual "office" that searches ad hoc for its officeholders or functionaries.

In this study, furthermore, it always remains unclear whether specific sacramental functions, for which priestly ordination is required, can also be carried out by laymen merely on the basis of an ecclesial commission without ordination. The entire approach is fundamentally flawed, because the author, while depending on *Lumen gentium* 28, misquotes it tendentiously. In his opinion, Vatican II relates divine

---

[45] Pope Innocent I, *Ep.* 2, 3; 25, 3; Council of Antioch, c. 10; Pope Gelasius I, *Ep.* 9, 6; 14, 6; Pope Leo the Great, *Serm.* 48, 1; John the Deacon, *Ep. ad Senarium* 7. The opinion of the Arian Aërius of Sebaste that there is complete equality between the episcopacy and the presbyterate was considered heretical; Epiphanius of Salamis, *Haer.* 74, 5; Augustine, *Haer.* 53. Despite a certain tradition in parts of the West that minimized the difference theologically (Ambrosiaster, Jerome, Pseudo-Jerome [*De septem ordinibus*], Isidore of Seville, and also John Chrysostom), the fact remains that of all the witnesses to the tradition down to Thomas (*Sent.* 4, d. 24, q. 3, a. 2, sol. 2) and Bonaventure (*Sent.* 4, d. 24, p. 2, a. 2, q. 3), not one disputes the dogma that only the bishop can confer sacramental Orders or thus that the unity of Holy Orders and of the Church has its sacramental foundation in the power to ordain.

institution only to ministry or "office" as a whole, while the Church
has the freedom to develop ministerial forms arbitrarily and thus to
confer sacramental authority upon nonsacramental offices as well. In
reality, the Council says that the *ministerium ecclesiasticum* is instituted
and carried out in various degrees of order, which from antiquity
are called bishop, presbyter, and deacon. The Council considers [a]
the continuation of the apostolic mission, which during the first and
second centuries became differentiated into various degrees, each of
which represents a participation in the mission of the apostles on
the basis of ordination, and [b] the terminology that only gradually
became generally accepted, which assigns to each of the degrees a
specific *terminus technicus*. The Council is quite clear in teaching that
the apostles gave to their successors a share in their own consecration
and mission and that the inner gradation [of Holy Orders] into presbyterate and diaconate resulted from the initiative of the apostles and
of the leaders of local churches in early Christian times. The main
flaw in all these attempts to lump together the service of sacramental
ministry and the offices created by Church law is their tendency to
obscure the sacramental structure of the Church, of the apostolate,
and of the threefold Sacrament of Holy Orders that has proceeded
from the apostolate. In those passages [of the dissertation] where sociological and pragmatic pastoral arguments threaten to overwhelm the
theological reasoning, there seems to be a confusion of ecclesiology
and sociology. Pastoral substructures that have developed in parts of
Western Europe, which have no theological justification, are now
supposed to gain legitimacy after the fact from the normative force of
the status quo, while the dogmatic and binding teaching of the Church
concerning the Sacrament of Holy Orders is relativized. This trend is
defended with an appeal to alleged ambiguities in tradition: e.g., the
gradually emerging threefold structure of the Sacrament of Orders
in the transition from the apostolic to the postapostolic age, which
is interpreted along purely sociological lines as the result of various
models of self-organization arbitrarily determined by the local communities. Further uncertainty is detected in later discussions about the
dogmatic difference between the presbyterate and the episcopacy, and
also in the similar names given to the diaconal ministry and the office
of the deaconess, which, contrary to the evidence in the sources, is
interpreted as being identical to the former. The *ius divinum* [divine

law] seems to be understood as purely historical organizational acts of institution performed by Jesus before the Resurrection. If their existence, as such, cannot be proved, then the conclusion is drawn that the three degrees of the Sacrament of Holy Orders are merely a matter of Church law. In reality this model, which is based on a facile contrast of suprahistorical truths and chance historical conditions, can in no way do justice to the historicity of revelation and the historicity of its tradition and definitive reception in the Church's profession of faith, which are postulated by a modern hermeneutic of dogma. (In terms of such a model, how can one reconcile, for example, the genesis of the scriptural canon, which took place in stages, with the reverence shown to Sacred Scripture from the very beginning as the *norma normans non normata* [the norm or rule that regulates but is not regulated])?

Evidence from the apostolic and postapostolic age

Evidence of an awareness of this problem can be found already in New Testament times. In "all the churches of the saints" (1 Cor 14:33–37) of the Pauline tradition, it is considered impermissible and unfitting—because of a "command of the Lord"—for women to speak "in church", that is, in the assembly. There is a reminder of the "law" that demands that they be subordinate and ask their husbands at home if they desire to know something. There is no doubt about the membership of women believers in the Church or about their participation in the assemblies (not only eucharistic ones). How the men ought to conduct themselves here is not mentioned. The prophetic speech of all the baptized who have this charism (1 Cor 11:4f.; 14:26–33) is equally suitable for men *and* women (within the assemblies or at home?). In particular, it remains unclear whether the "prohibition" against women speaking is an ad hoc disciplinary measure or a statement of principle.

The apostolic ministry of the "message of reconciliation

... [as] ambassadors for Christ" (2 Cor 5:19–20) should be distinguished from charismatic testimony and from the sort of speech about the faith that remains possible and desirable down to this present day in the church community and the worship assembly. When Paul justifies the prohibition against women speaking with the rhetorical question, "What! Did the word of God originate with you, or are you the only ones it has reached?" (1 Cor 14:36), then he is not singling out and addressing women, for the Word of God did not proceed from the men of the Corinthian community either, but rather from the apostles Paul, Cephas, and Apollos, who proclaimed the gospel to them (cf. 1 Cor 1:2–17). It is obvious that Paul (precisely with a view to the following verse, 1 Cor 14:37) is proving the legitimacy of his instruction from his apostolic authority as one who is formally empowered to proclaim the gospel, which became the principle by which the Church, her ministries, offices, and charisms were formed.

The meaning of this Pauline instruction becomes clearer in the pastoral letters. There is no doubt about the contribution of women in handing on the teachings of the faith in the family and in their circle of acquaintances (1 Tim 3:11; 2 Tim 1:5; Tit 2:4), about special positions of service held by women (1 Tim 5:9ff.), or about their vocation to evangelize and care for souls. In the list of moral exhortations for men and women, which Paul offers on his apostolic authority, it says, among other things, "I permit no woman to teach (*didaskein*)" (1 Tim 2:12); considering the context, however, this cannot be meant as the antithesis to a general *permission* for all men (as laymen) to do so. The public ministry of the Word and of teaching is the province of the bishop and the presbyters, by virtue of their participation in the apostolic

Magisterium, to which they have been appointed through the imposition of hands. The implicit message, rather, is that women are not called to the Magisterium or to the ministry of leadership exercised by the shepherds (bishops and presbyters). The Apostle is opposing the custom that had crept into the early Gnostic communities: that women —who were among the protagonists of that heretical movement—claimed the ministry of teaching and governing as their own.

The real distinction, however, is only inadequately expressed by the pair of concepts, "public/private". Apostolic *kerygma* and preaching is a matter of proclaiming the gospel authoritatively, whereas the charisms of interpreting and announcing it and of helping to build up the Church (in the sense of the common participation in the priestly-prophetic mission of the Universal Church) follow from the commission that all the faithful should become "stewards of God's various grace[s]" and gifts for each other's benefit (cf. 1 Pet 4:10).

Finally, Sacred Scripture records only in a general way the will of the Lord and the instruction of the apostles, which is reflected in the practice of the early Church. We do not find speculative reasoning and explanations. The admonition to wives to be subordinate to their husbands according to the mind of Christ (whereby the husband for his part has to take Christ's kenotic [self-emptying] love as the model for his conduct toward his wife and family) concerns the system of personal relationships within marriage only. By no means does this appeal, to be conformed to the mind of Christ the Servant, imply a general subordination of women in the Christian community, much less a biological, ontological, or theological inferiority of baptized women with respect to men in the lay state. The exact opposite is true, in contrast to the early Gnostic movements, even those within the Christian communities.

Therefore citing an allegedly essential inability of women to teach or to lead cannot serve as an explanation to justify the fact that women are not ordained.

Evidence from the patristic age of the Church's beliefs

In many commentaries of the Church Fathers[46] and medieval theologians on 1 Corinthians 14:33–37 and 1 Timothy 2:11, only the positive command of Christ is derived from these passages. Any reference to a "subordination" (not an inferiority), whether understood in a soteriological or in a natural sense, is only mentioned as an additional explanation. Nowhere does nonadmission to ordination follow as a conclusion from the premise that a woman is less fully human in some social or ontological-creaturely way.

It was not an anthropological misjudgment that led to a deliberate or incidental exclusion of women from the Sacrament of Holy Orders. Rather, the Church believed that, according to the command of Christ and of the apostles, ordained ministry can be exercised only by men called to do so; it was this faith, expressed in the Church's practice, that led to the search for exegetical reasons and to anthropological considerations. Therefore determining the presence of an inadequate anthropology does not deprive the Church's practice of a sound basis.

[46] Cf. Origen, *In 1 Cor.* 14:34–35, ed. Jenkins, in *Journal of Theological Studies* 10 (1909): 41f.; cf. the French translation in Roger Gryson, *Le Ministère des femmes dans l'Église ancienne,* Recherches et synthèses, section d'histoire, 4 (Gembloux, 1972), pp. 57f. The book cites other pertinent passages; see the index.

The practice of the Church from the very beginnings cannot be explained as a carry-over from the sociological model of the *oikos* [household], headed by the *pater familias*. This is evident from the fact that by no means all bishops and presbyters were simultaneously heads of households that had become Christian, and, conversely, fathers who headed households were not per se leaders of the churches. Many apostles and itinerant missionaries were devoted to "the affairs of the Lord" (1 Cor 7:32; Mt 19:12; Lk 18:28); they were celibate and poor and thus without ties to a "household". In the pastoral letters (for instance in 1 Tim 3:1–7) we are dealing with criteria of aptitude.

In the early Christian communities (just as throughout Church history) there were leading spiritual and intellectual personalities in the lay state, among them women who headed the *oikos* of antiquity, who most certainly were not bishops or presbyters in their local churches: we can name here Martha and Mary (Lk 10:38–39), Lydia of Thyatira (Acts 16:14), Nympha (Col 4:15), or Prisca with her husband Aquila (1 Cor 16:19; Acts 18:2; 2 Tim 4:19).

Hippolytus of Rome (*Trad. apost.* 10) and the Council of Nicaea (can. 19), in emphasizing that inclusion in the roll of widows and conferral of the office of lector and subdeacon do not take place through the sacramental imposition of hands by which one becomes a bishop, presbyter, or deacon, not only clarify the difference between ordained ministry and the other ecclesial offices, but also indirectly confirm that only men received and can receive sacramental Orders. It was only a question of terminology, if occasionally the term *clerus* (ministry, order) was used in a wider sense and could also include other ecclesial offices besides the degrees of Holy Orders of the bishop, the presbyter, and the deacon. At any rate it furnishes no argument to the contrary, if in a few regions the rite of blessing through the imposition of hands was carried out on the occasion of other sacraments and sacramentals, for instance at the installation of a deaconess (the superior of a convent), of a subdeacon, a lector, etc. (*Const. apost.* 8, 19, 1f.; Chalcedon, can. 15). The real difference becomes evident in the prayer of consecration and in the statement of the specific services entailed in each degree of consecration or ordination. If the deaconess and the subdeacon are not allowed to carry out the duties of the presbyter or the deacon, then they have not received such a commission in their blessing or consecration either, and thus they *are* not deacons.[47]

To what extent the connection between the Sacrament of Holy Orders and baptized men as recipients was perceived as part of apostolic tradition and hence as something belonging to the substance of the Sacrament of Orders (*per sensum fidei*) becomes especially clear when we ask whether customs of certain groups that deviated from the *praxis Ecclesiae* were considered heretical and thus contrary to the Church's profession of faith. The faith of the Church on this matter is expressed not only in a verbal profession, but also in the liturgical practice (*lex orandi—lex credendi*; DH 246).

Representing the mind of the Church in the second and third centuries are authors such as Irenaeus of Lyons,[48] Hippolytus,[49] Clement of Alexandria,[50] Origen,[51] Tertullian,[52] and Cyprian.[53] We cannot always make out precisely what the particular teaching and practice may have been in the Gnostic sects, the fanatical movements, and the heretical positions that these authors opposed. The belief of the Church

[47] Cf. *Const. apost.* 5, 28, 6; Epiphanius, *Haer.* 79, 2; *Expositio fidei* 21; cf. Hans Jorissen, "Theologische Bedenken gegen die Diakonatsweihe von Frauen", in: Hünermann, *Diakonat,* pp. 86–97.

[48] *Haer.* 1, 13, 2.

[49] *Trad. apost.* 10.

[50] *Paidagogos* 3, 12, 97; *Strom.* 3, 6, 52, 3–5.

[51] *In 1 Cor.* 14:34–35 (Jenkins, JThS 10:41f.).

[52] *Praescr.* 41; *Bapt.* 17; *Virg. veland.* 9.

[53] *Ep.* 63. Letter from Bishop Firmilian of Caesarea to Cyprian of Carthage (among the letters of Cyprian), *Ep.* 75, 10.

Fathers with regard to their understanding of the Church, nevertheless, comes to light: that there is, above and beyond the common priesthood in which all baptized men and women participate, a special apostolic ministry of proclaiming the gospel, a sanctifying ministry of celebrating the liturgy and administering the sacraments, and a pastoral ministry. This ministry can be conferred legitimately, in the degrees of bishop, presbyter, and deacon, upon men only, and only men can exercise it. Occasionally, when recourse is had to the suitability argument, this should be understood in the traditional way (so as not to attract the attention of the pagans), rather than as an assimilation of pagan religious customs and forms of their cultic temple worship of the gods.[54] For the ministry of proclaiming and shepherding, as well as the presidency at the eucharistic meal (as a re-presentation, in the Word, of Christ's death and Resurrection), would have been unrecognizable to the pagans and could in no way (neither in its external form nor as to its christological content) have been considered comparable to their sacrificial priesthood and their sacrificial rituals.

In the view of the authors of the fourth and fifth centuries, who represent the tradition of the Universal Church, it was the Cataphrygians,[55] an offshoot of the Montanists (also called Pepuzianists) who called into question the *praxis Ecclesiae* and the *consensus fidei* with regard to the legitimate

---

[54] Rosemarie Nürnberg, "Non decet neque necessarium est, ut mulieres doceant", JbAC 31 (1988): 57–73; Ernst Dassmann, "Die frühchristliche Tradition über den Ausschluss der Frauen vom Priesteramt", in idem, *Ämter und Dienste in den frühchristlichen Gemeinden* (Bonn, 1994), pp. 212–24; idem, "Non decet neque necessarium est. . . . Die frühchristliche Tradition über den Ausschluss der Frauen vom Priesteramt und dem Dienst der Verkündigung", in *Kleine Bonner Theologische Reihe: Vorträge—Aufsätze—Stellungnahmen* (Bonn, 1997), pp. 52–65.

[55] Cf. Eusebius of Caesarea, *Hist. eccl.* 5, 18.

recipient of the Sacrament of Orders. It would be putting the cart before the horse to conclude, from the unanimous rejection of this idea *as* a heresy, that the heretics had continued an old tradition of the Church and that it was only an anti-heretical animus that prompted the Church Fathers to throw it overboard, along with the heretics and several other old Catholic traditions.

This sort of detective work, which extracts from the sources the exact opposite of what they say literally, is refuted also by the fact that not one single text by a Catholic author confirms the presence, in the Catholic Church, of the allegedly Catholic practice that was supposedly then given up as part of a strategy for marginalizing heretics who appeared later.

After all, the Church Fathers do not criticize the fact that women (martyrs, women who lead a holy life and have prophetic gifts) appear in positions of spiritual and intellectual leadership in the Church[56] or the fact that women in the Church possess the charism of prophetic speech or even hold ecclesial offices (enrolled widows, deaconesses, etc.).[57]

As for the alleged misogyny of the Church Fathers, we present the following text of John Chrysostom, a commentary on Romans 16:5f.

How is this? a woman again is honored and proclaimed victorious! Again are we men put to shame. Or rather, we are not put to shame only, but have even an honor conferred upon us. For an honor we have, in that there are such women amongst us, but we are put to shame, in that we men are left so far behind by them. But if we come to know whence it comes, that they are so adorned, we too shall speedily overtake them. Whence then is their adorning? Let both men and women listen. It is not from bracelets, or from necklaces, nor from their eunuchs either, and

[56] Chrysostom, *In Rom. hom.* 32 (on Rom 16:7).
[57] Origen, *In Rom.* 16:1.

their maid-servants, and gold-broidered dresses, but from their
toils in behalf of the truth. For he says, "[she,] who bestowed
much labor on us," that is, not on herself only, nor upon her
own advancement, (for this many women of the present day do,
by fasting, and sleeping on the floor), but upon others also, so
carrying on the race Apostles and Evangelists ran. In what sense
then does [the Apostle] say, "I suffer not a woman to teach"?
(1 Tim 2:12). He means to hinder her from publicly coming forward (1 Cor 14:35), and from the seat on the bema [rostrum],
not from the word of teaching. Since if this were the case, how
would he have said to the woman that had an unbelieving husband, "How knowest thou, O woman, if thou shalt save thy husband?" (1 Cor 7:16). Or how came he to suffer her to admonish
children, when he says, but "she shall be saved by child-bearing if
they continue in faith, and charity, and holiness, with sobriety?"
(1 Tim 2:15). How came Priscilla to instruct even Apollos? It was
not then to cut in sunder private conversing for advantage that
[Paul] said this, but that [which took place] before all, and which
it was the teacher's duty to give in the public assembly; or again,
in case the husband be believing and thoroughly furnished, able
also to instruct her. When she is the wiser, then he does not for-
bid her teaching and improving him. And [the Apostle] does not
say, who taught much, but "who bestowed much labor," because
along with teaching [του λόγου] she performs other ministries besides, those in the way of dangers, in the way of money, in the way
of travels. For the women of those days were more spirited than
lions, sharing with the Apostles their labors for the Gospel's sake.
In this way they went travelling with them, and also performed
all other ministries. And even in Christ's day there followed Him
women, "which ministered unto Him of their substance" (Lk
8:3), and waited upon the Teacher.[58]

What the Church Fathers object to, rather, is that in the
sects, the ministry of the bishop or the presbyter is conferred
upon women or claimed by them, *contrary to* the beliefs of the

[58] *In Rom. hom.* 32, *Nicene and Post-Nicene Fathers*, 1st series, vol. 11,
ed. Philip Schaff (Peabody, Mass.: Hendrickson Pubs., 1995), p. 554; cf.
earlier Origen, *In Rom.* 16:7 (FC 2/5, pp. 243f.).

Catholic Church.[59] Why should the Catholic Church suddenly remove women from the ministries of bishop, presbyter, and deacon simply because women were considered to be prophetesses among the Montanists? The criticism did not concern the prophetic speech of women, but rather the claim of men and women that they were supplementing or invalidating the *traditio apostolica* with their private revelations and unmediated illuminations. The only possible connection would be, at most, that purportedly prophetic speech of men and women was subsequently treated with more caution.

No arguments about an allegedly natural inferiority of women are marshaled, so as to derive from them new maxims for a Church policy of excluding women from sacramental Orders. Rather, the heretics are countered with references to the positive will of Christ, the example of his actions and those of the early Church, and the so-called "teaching prohibition" of the Apostle (1 Cor 14; 1 Tim 2).[60] Only to make

[59] Cf. here Rudolph, *Die Gnosis*, p. 229: "The percentage of women was evidently very high and shows that Gnosticism gave them opportunities that were otherwise denied them, especially in the official Church. In many cases they took on positions of leadership, whether as teachers, prophetesses, missionaries, or as those who conducted cultic ceremonies (Baptism, Eucharist) and magical procedures (exorcisms). A certain Marcellina, for example, spread the doctrines of Karpokrates around A.D. 150 in Rome. Ptolemaios, an important disciple of Valentinus, wrote a detailed letter, which has come down to us, about questions of interpreting the Mosaic Law, to an educated woman addressee, whom he calls 'Sister Flora'." Cf. also Jerome, *Ep.* 41 to Marcella.

[60] A comprehensive collection of all the texts relevant to the problem of deaconesses and their office is presented by Josephine Mayer, ed., *Monumenta de viduis diaconissis virginibusque tractantia* (Bonn, 1938). Martimort shows that the office of the deaconess in the early Church was not understood in a sacramental sense: Aimé Georges Martimort, *Deaconesses: An Historical Study*, trans. by K. D. Whitehead (San Francisco : Ignatius Press, 1986).

this more comprehensible do writers (not always) have recourse to anthropological considerations.

Ambrosiaster (around A.D. 380) observes with regard to
1 Timothy 3:11:

> Because the Apostle addresses women after the deacons, the
> Cataphrygians seize upon this as an opportunity for heresy
> and with vain arrogance maintain that the deaconesses, too,
> must have been ordained; even though they know that the
> apostles selected seven men as deacons. Could they not find,
> on that occasion, any suitable woman, since we read that
> there were holy women with the twelve apostles? (Cf. Acts
> 1:14). . . . Yet the Apostle orders women to be silent in the
> assembly of the faithful.[61]

Epiphanius of Salamis, in his anti-heretical work *Panarion*
[The medicine chest] (composed around 374–377), reckons
the teaching and practice of the Phrygians among the heresies: "They allow women to hold the offices of shepherd and
priest."[62] In opposing the Montanists he cites the prohibition against speaking (1 Cor 14:34) and the more precisely
worded "prohibition against teaching" (1 Tim 2:12) and
accuses the heretics of disregarding the instructions of the
Apostle. As for those who erroneously argue from an alleged
intellectual superiority of women—Eve, after all, ate from
the tree of knowledge—and the evidence of women proph-
esying in the Old Testament, and the abolition of the difference between the sexes (citing Gal 3:28), as well as from
the Montanist prophetess Priscilla, who claimed to have
had a vision of Christ in the form of a woman,[63] Epiphanius

---

[61] *In 1 Tim.* 3, CSEL, 81, 3. [Translated from German.]
[62] Cf. Epiphanius, *Anakephalaiosis* 49 (BKV, 38, 208). [Translated from German.]
[63] *Haer.* 49, 3.

responds with a lapidary remark: "Nowhere (in the Old Testament) did a woman serve as a priestess."[64]

A further argument consists in the observation that even Mary was not entrusted with the priestly ministry.

> If women were meant to be authorized by God to hold the priestly office, then no one in the New Testament would have been more worthy than Mary to exercise the priestly ministry. . . . She was clothed with such great honor that she was permitted to prepare a dwelling place in her womb for the God of heaven and King of all, the Son of God. . . . Yet he did not deem it good to confer the priesthood upon her. He did not even entrust to her the task of baptizing; otherwise Christ should have been baptized by her instead of by John.[65]

In one of the first[66] thematic treatises "On the Priesthood" (ca. 385), one which has a lasting importance, John Chrysostom states that the priestly office, which is founded upon the bestowal of the office of chief shepherd upon Peter, can only be conferred upon baptized males. The related tasks of governing, teaching, and liturgical service could certainly be performed by many men and women who are capable of them. "But when one is required to preside over the Church, and to be entrusted with the care of so many souls, the whole female sex must retire before the magnitude of the task, and the majority of men also."[67]

The "awe-inspiring" dignity of the priesthood results

---

[64] Ibid. 79, 3.

[65] Ibid. [Translated here from German.] The same reasoning is found in Augustine, "Zur Ehrung der Frau" [In honor of woman] from: *Serm. Denis.* 25, 4 (Franz Courth, *Mariologie*, Texte zur Theologie, 6 [Graz/Vienna/Cologne, 1991], p. 90).

[66] Preceded chiefly by the second theological discourse of Gregory Nazianzen; cf. Manfred Lachbrunner, *Über das Priestertum: Historische und systematische Untersuchung zum Priesterbild des Johannes Chrysostomus,* Hereditas, 5 (Bonn, 1993), pp. 39–66.

[67] *Sac.* 2, 2.

from the fact that mortal men[68] are called to represent Christ in his Person and in his self-sacrificial service, to mediate salvation, and, like the Good Shepherd, to lay down their lives for the people. Although the "divine law" has excluded women from the priesthood, many seek admission by using force or try to set themselves up as rulers over the priests of the Church and to have them at their beck and call, like slaves.[69] Yet, according to Chrysostom, Paul did not allow them to teach in the assembly of the Church, indeed, not even to speak or to rule over their husbands.

For Jerome[70] and Augustine[71] the teaching of the Montanists (Priscillianists, Pepuzianists, Quintilianists), according to which women could hold the offices of bishop and priest, was tantamount to heresy.

John Damascene (d. around 750), who synthesizes the entire doctrinal development of the East and thus of the entire Church in antiquity as well, included the erroneous teachings of the Pepuzianists or the Quintilianists in his catalogue of heresies.[72]

On one important occasion Pope Gelasius I, in a letter to the bishops of Champagne (491), gives expression to the doctrinal consensus of the Church with regard to abuses: "As We have heard, to Our chagrin, such a disregard for divine truths has become common, that even women, so it is reported, serve on the holy altars; and everything that is entrusted exclusively to the service of men is carried out by the sex to which it is not befitting."[73]

In the year 511 the bishops of Gaul vent their indignation

[68] Ibid. 3, 5.
[69] Ibid. 3, 9.
[70] *Ep.* 41, 4.
[71] *Haer.* 27.
[72] John Damascene, *Liber de Haeresibus* 49; Müller, *Quellen*, p. 256.
[73] *Ep.* 9, 26. [Translated from German.]

in a letter about the innovation and the unheard-of superstition of one sect (named after their founder, Pepodius) that admits women to service at the altar. Any adherents to this error are excluded from the eucharistic community.[74]

Similar statements are made by many councils, which expressly reject the admission of women, in any shape or form whatsoever beyond the *ordines minores*, to the sacramental diaconate, presbyterate, or episcopacy.[75]

Evidence of the Church's beliefs in the Middle Ages and the modern era

Medieval and modern theology in its entirety[76] adopts the doctrinal opinion of the Universal Church that by a *divine command* women cannot be admitted to the priesthood and condemns the opposing view of the Waldensians[77] and Wycliffites[78] as a heresy.

Two popes, Innocent III and Innocent IV, confirm the Church's practice as the authentic expression of the Church's faith.[79]

[74] Letter of three Gallic bishops (A.D. 511), in Müller, *Quellen*, pp. 102–4.

[75] Synod of Laodicea (late fourth century), cann. 11 and 45; Carthage (398), can. 99; Orange (441), can. 26; Epaôn (517), can. 21; Orléans (533), can. 18; Synod at Aachen (789), can. 17; Synod at Paris (829), can. 45. All texts are found in Müller, *Quellen*.

[76] Ludwig Ott, *Das Weihesakrament*, HDG 4/5 (Freiburg, 1969), pp. 108f., 165f.

[77] Cf. Hermann Schuster and Hermann Schürmann, *Christentum in Geschichte und Gegenwart* (Frankfurt a.M./Bonn, 1950), pp. 63f.

[78] Cf. Thomas Netter, O.Carm. (ca. 1377–1431), known as Thomas Waldensis, *Doctrinale antiquitatum fidei catholicae ecclesiae* 3; Müller, *Quellen*, pp. 120–26.

[79] Innocent III, Decretal *Nova quaedam* (1210), Friedberg 2:886f.; Innocent IV, *Commentaria Apparatus in V libros Decretalium* (Frankfurt, 1570; facsimile reprinting, Frankfurt, 1968), p. 545.

Only in the twentieth century, since the 1970s, have there been more and more voices calling into question the theological status of the traditional teaching that only a baptized male can receive Holy Orders validly.

Nevertheless, for the tradition of dogmatic and canonical teaching, taken as a whole, it is certain that *ex necessitate sacramenti* the male sex of the recipient is a constitutive element (*de substantia sacramenti*) in the worthy reception of the Sacrament of Holy Orders and that this therefore belongs to the unalterable substance of the sacrament.

A long series of papal statements and council decisions[80] of a theological and disciplinary nature confirms that we are not merely dealing here with a theological tradition of the schools, but rather that the theological and canonical documents reflect the constant teaching of the ordinary Magisterium; this teaching is presented in such a way that it must be viewed as belonging to the substance of the sacrament and therefore believed to be something originating in a divine decree. The contrary teaching is rejected as heretical.

The corresponding canons of the CIC [Code of Canon Law] of 1917 and 1983, as well as the discussion from *Inter insigniores*, are taken up and clarified by Pope John Paul II in section 4 of *Ordinatio sacerdotalis*, in which he states with precision the traditional Catholic doctrine, which is binding in faith:

> Although the teaching that priestly ordination is to be reserved to men alone has been preserved by the constant and universal Tradition of the Church and firmly taught by the Magisterium in its more recent documents, at the present

---

[80] The *Decretum Gratiani* (Friedberg 1:750) summarizes the tradition: "Mulieres autem non solum ad sacerdotium, sed nec etiam ad diaconatum provehi possunt" [Women cannot be promoted to the priesthood; not only that, but not even to the diaconate].

time in some places it is nonetheless considered still open to debate, or the Church's judgment that women are not to be admitted to ordination is considered to have a merely disciplinary force.

Wherefore, in order that all doubt may be removed regarding a matter of great importance, a matter which pertains to the Church's divine constitution itself, in virtue of my ministry of confirming the brethren (cf. Lk 22:32) I declare that the Church has no authority whatsoever to confer priestly ordination on women and that this judgment is to be definitively held by all the Church's faithful.

3.7 *The suitability arguments of classical theology for the* praxis Ecclesiae

Parallel with the emergence of sacramental doctrine since the middle of the twelfth century and the beginnings of systematic theology in general (in the schools of the religious orders and universities), a systematic treatment[81] of the question about the valid recipient of the Sacrament of Orders also develops. What had often been mentioned previously only in an incidental way and ad hoc, is now elaborated in the context of the systematic method of theology. For the canonical tradition it is certain that the practice of the Church is anchored in divine law, i.e., in the institutional will of Jesus, and that it is not a question of a merely disciplinary law of custom.

The great Scholastics generally treat the question con-

---

[81] On the Scholastic theologians, cf. Ott, *Weihesakrament*, pp. 108f. In the seventeenth century see the very thorough and astonishingly relevant work of François Hallier (1595–1659), *De sacris Electionibus et Ordinationibus, ex antiquo et novo Ecclesiae usu* (1636); J. P. Migne, ed., *Cursus Theologiae completus* 24, columns 821–54 (available also in German in: Müller, *Quellen*, pp. 361–73).

cerning the conditions for receiving the Sacrament of Holy Orders in their commentaries on the *Sentences* of Peter Lombard (lib. 4, d. 25), and as a rule they mention, besides being baptized and an adult, being of the male sex also.[82]

The relation between positive and speculative grounds

The unanimous rejection of the doctrinal opinion of the Cataphrygians as a heresy in the strict sense of the word is decisive. It is a question of contradicting the Church's teaching and not just deviating from her discipline. Conversely, assent to the Church's teaching means this: that ordination to the episcopacy, presbyterate, or diaconate, conferred upon a woman by a legitimate bishop, is invalid, not only *de iure* (*ecclesiastico*) [= by law (of the Church)] and de facto, but also *ex necessitate substantiae sacramenti* [necessarily by virtue of the substance of the sacrament], that is to say, *de iure divino* [by divine law].

Everyone sees the Church's practice and teaching as having their real basis in the biblical prohibition against women teaching in church or ruling over their husbands. All commentaries on 1 Corinthians 14 and 1 Timothy 2, in continu-

[82] We can disregard the interpretation by the canonists and the Scholastics of language about the *diaconissa* or *presbytera* (*episcopa*), which appears in many old canons and is further transmitted via the *Decretum Gratiani*, since it concerned either the wives of the respective ordained ministers (cann. 13, 19, 20 of the Council of Tours, A.D. 567; can. 21 of the Council of Auxerre, A.D. 585), or else the superiors of spiritual institutes or convents (thus Gregory of Nyssa, *Vita Macrinae*, BKV 56, 360; Egeria, *Itinerarium* 2), whereas with the office of deaconess (as in the earlier case of the enrolled widows), it is a question of providing auxiliary services during the Baptism of women—for instance performing the anointings —or of assisting in the pastoral care of women for reasons of propriety, or else of providing in an official capacity for the poor of the congregation (*Const. apost.* 8, 28).

ity with the Church Fathers, present this reading as the authentic interpretation of Christ's institutional will. Although most Scholastics concentrate on the power to consecrate as the defining feature of priestly orders, they still do not lose sight of the ministry of teaching and shepherding that is essentially connected with the priesthood. Apostolic teaching authority, the command at the Last Supper to celebrate the eucharistic memorial, the authority to forgive sins handed over by the risen Lord, together with Jesus' ministry as Shepherd, were all given to the apostles alone, and they were men. For this reason women cannot receive the priestly ordination that is bound up with these powers. As far as teaching authority is concerned, women are expressly disqualified.

The unanimous practice of the Church proves the authenticity of this interpretation. The theologians of the Middle Ages and the modern era are, in this connection, witnesses to the *universal* belief of the Church. They stand in agreement with the ordinary Magisterium, which proposes this teaching as something revealed by God.

To that extent, the speculative justification, which can vary in character from one particular text to another, builds upon the positive nature of the Church's belief. Considerations of an anthropological sort do not lead to the exclusion of women from Holy Orders. The real reason for the conditions for validity is not based upon theological and anthropological conclusions or upon cultural and sociological customs and thought patterns. Rather, all theological expositions of the Sacrament of Holy Orders proceed from the certainty, in faith, that the Church's teaching and practice carry out the institutional will of Christ and are rooted in it, and thus are normative, prior to any and all speculative elucidation.

In the speculative justification, two levels of argumentation emerge: one dealing with sacramental theology and a

second that is anthropological (which means here the doctrine of a natural or postlapsarian *status subjectionis*). The two
levels do not necessarily go together.

So, for example, John Duns Scotus,[83] Durandus,[84] Petrus
de Palude,[85] and Wendelin Steinbach[86] by and large disregard
the secondary argument about why women lack the qualifications to teach and govern. Duns Scotus, for instance,
expressly states that the Church by her own authority could
not have excluded the entire female sex from the priesthood
unless this arrangement originated with Christ himself and
thus was of divine right.[87] Harking back to the patristic argument regarding the all-surpassing sanctity and fullness of
grace of Mary, the Mother of God,[88] who is the most noble
member of the Church, it is explained that Mary did not
receive the apostolic ministry and with it the priesthood because the free and express institutional will of Jesus provided
only for men to be recipients of the Sacrament of Holy Orders.

In Thomas Aquinas and Bonaventure, too, one can ob-

[83] Ox. 4 *Sent.* d. 25, q. 2, *Joannis Duns Scoti Opera* 24 (Paris, 1894), pp.
369f.

[84] *Sent.* 4, d. 25, q. 2, 1–6 (fol. 314b–c).

[85] Ibid. 4, d. 25, q. 3, a. 1, concl. 1 (fol. 134b–c).

[86] *Suppl.* d. 25, a. 2, concl. 9 (fol. 32c).

[87] "I do not believe, namely, that any office useful for salvation has
been withheld from any person through institution by the Church or
prescription of the apostles, and much less still from an entire existing
sex. If, then, the apostles or the Church cannot justly withhold from a
person any office useful for salvation unless Christ, as their head, has
so determined, and much less still from the entire female sex, therefore
Christ alone first prescribed this, he who instituted the sacrament." (Ox.
4 *Sent.* d. 25, q. 2 quoted in Manfred Hauke, *Women in the Priesthood: A
Systematic Analysis in the Light of the Order of Creation and Redemption*, trans.
David Kipp [San Francisco, 1988], p. 455).

[88] Duns Scotus, Ox. 4 *Sent.* d. 25, q. 2. Cf. the early statements of
Epiphanius, Augustine, and also of Innocent III and the decretal of Gregory IX, *Nova quaedam* (Corpus, ed. Friedberg 2:886f.).

serve the primacy of the positive justification, as a matter of divine law, over the speculative justification. Within the speculative argumentation, reasons from sacramental theology have priority over those from the perspective of natural law.

Since the priest, in his own person, represents Christ—and this not by the mere fact that he is of the male sex, but rather in the symbolic representation of the relation of Christ to the Church (Head-Body, Bridegroom-Bride), which has its foundations in the polarity of human sexuality and is rooted in the masculinity of Jesus Christ, the incarnate Word and human Mediator—the priest needs more than just the conferral of authority. Being the sacramental representation of this salvific relationship of Christ to the Church and of his marital union with her, he must resemble Christ. Accordingly, the male or female sex is not an accidental quality like race, color, age, or state of health. These either play no part at all in the worthy reception of the Sacrament of Orders, or else, as for example with some health issues, present merely disciplinary impediments to Orders that can be dispensed from at any time.

Consequently there is no point to the populist argument that the Church, which has admitted not only Jewish fishermen but also Roman officials and Bavarian farm boys to Holy Orders, can impose hands on women, too, and ordain them. The difference between the sexes has its foundations in creation. God created man as male and female, but not as fisherfolk, officials, or farmers. When Medard Kehl, for instance, writes that the Church, atypically, still clings to a natural distinguishing feature (e.g., sex, education, race, social status, nationality) only in the case of Holy Orders,[89] we need to recall that the distinction between man and woman is not one of the many accidental circumstances in which man lives, but is rather an essential determination of a human being's existence in history, both individually and

[89] Medard Kehl, *Die Kirche: Eine katholische Ekklesiologie* (Würzburg, 1992), pp. 457f.

as part of society. Upon this distinction is founded nothing less than the sacramental character of marriage and the mystery of the intimate communion of Christ as Bridegroom with the Church, his Bride (cf. LG 4).

In the personal complementarity of husband and wife, the primordial symbolism of creation comes to the fore, in which God's personal mediation and communication of himself as Creator, Redeemer, and Sanctifier of man (as person in communion) is indicated and realized.

The position of St. Thomas received particular attention in the following centuries because he, like Bonaventure and Duns Scotus, was the founder of a school and remained a point of reference, not only for all later Summas, theological manuals, and commentaries on the *Sentences*, but also for commentaries on 1 Corinthians 14 and 1 Timothy 2.

Presuppositions in the argumentation of Thomas Aquinas

Thomas' doctrine about the relation between man and woman is very closely connected with his justification of the association between priestly ordination and the male sex; both have been sharply criticized on many occasions in the recent debate. With the "misogyny of Aquinas", the "traditional hatred of women" found in the Catholic Church allegedly reached its absolute nadir.[90]

In order to gain a proper perspective for an objective interpretation of an earlier form of theology, it is important to note first that Thomas—like all medieval Doctors of the Church—did not derive his theology from a storehouse of personal experiences and allow his biography to be reflected

[90] Thus Peter Ketsch, *Frauen im Mittelalter* (Düsseldorf, 1984), p. 65; cf. the contrary analysis, based upon a knowledge of the texts, by Alfons Hufnagel, "Die Bewertung der Frau bei Thomas von Aquin", ThQ 156 (1976): 133–47.

in it. He retreats behind his work as a commentator in a Scholastic tradition and remains committed to its objective structure of argumentation, which draws upon Scripture and the authority of the Fathers and rationally interprets them.[91] Nothing is methodologically more misguided than to try to explain doctrinal positions of Scholastic theologians as the result of psychological dispositions. Since the inner development of most of the authors is scarcely known, attempts to reduce theological theses to psychological influences amount to sheer speculations on shaky grounds.

Furthermore, the opinion that the life of a monk or of a priest could only result from a profound disturbance with regard to the female sex, which inevitably manifests itself in "misogyny" disguised with philosophical and theological arguments, ought to be questioned in turn as to its objective validity and the psychological background of its adherents. Christian celibacy, an evangelical way of life, does not spring from a neurotic fear of the opposite sex and does not manifest itself in an oppressive denial of sexual drives. It is a charismatic imitation of Christ's way of life, an intentional availability for service in the Kingdom of God (Mt 19:12). It is service in "the affairs of the Lord" (1 Cor 7:32), in caring for the salvation of one's neighbor and for the building up of the Church. In a culture where the female sex is viewed predominantly from the (archaic, naturalistic) perspective of producing offspring and satisfying desires, there is a greater danger of exploiting women than in a view of man as a being created in the image and likeness of God, which finds confirmation in man's personhood and capacity for interrelation. For man and woman exist as persons, and "person" designates the perfection of an individual, a

---

[91] For instance, *Suppl.* 39, 1 ad 1.

perfection that nothing in creation can surpass, which is realized in a rationally endowed nature.[92]

Someone who says, "Woman is not born, but made by
society" (Simone de Beauvoir), denies woman (in effect,
however unwittingly) any absolute identity of her own. According to the Christian understanding, this identity belongs
to her as an inalienable gift from God by the very fact that
she is a creature. Scholasticism may know nothing about the
genetic reasons for the difference between the sexes, but it
does start its anthropology with the theology of creation and
of grace, and to that extent it is more human-friendly, and
thus woman-friendly as well, than the program for emanci-
pating the "new man" through self-creation.

As far as being is concerned, woman is no different from
man, since she possesses a human soul just as he does and
in many instances displays better qualities of character than
many men.[93] As to the personhood, full membership in the
Church, reception of grace, and personal, immediate relationship with God that belong to all believers by virtue of
their spiritual priesthood, there is not the slightest doubt in
the works of Thomas (among other authors, but especially
so). All this is an article of faith. To dilute these truths in
any way would be heresy. This is evident also in sacramental
theology, since "either man or woman can baptize in a case
of urgency."[94]

[92] ST 1, 29, 3: "Persona significat id quod est perfectissimum in tota
natura subsistens in rationali natura" [Person signifies that which is most
perfect in all of creation, subsisting in a rational nature].

[93] *Suppl.* 39, 1 ad 1.

[94] Cf. ST 3, 67, 4 ad 1. "Just as a woman is not suffered to teach
in public, but is allowed to instruct and admonish privately; so she is
not permitted to baptize publicly and solemnly, and yet she can baptize
in a case of urgency." Cf. ST 3, 55, 1 ad 3: "A woman is not to be
allowed to teach publicly in church; but she may be permitted to give

Theologically, too, the real test of whether the identity and relatedness of man and woman have been explained correctly, in a way consistent with the theology of creation and of grace, is always the sacramental character of marriage. Even though Thomas could not explain accurately, in biological terms, the origins of the difference between the sexes —nor could any scholar before the beginning of the nineteenth century—and he described a girl as *mas occasio-natus* [a "conditioned" male] (inasmuch as the origin of the female sex is traced back to an external, "chance" circumstance, which supposedly caused the exception to the rule that the male [intrinsically] passes on his own sex when he begets), he still emphasized theologically, in view of the comprehensive plan of creation, that the female sex is an authentic expression of humanity. One consequence of creation theology is a conflict with Gnostic dualism, which assumes that the female is the lesser form of humanity, because of the allegedly greater proximity of woman (*mater—materia*) to the material world, whereas the male is thought to be closer to the spiritual world. This opposition can be resolved within

---

familiar instruction to some privately. And therefore as Ambrose says on Luke xxiv. 22, *a woman is sent to them who are of her household*, but not to the people to bear witness to the Resurrection. But Christ appeared to the woman first, for this reason, that as a woman was the first to bring the source of death to man, so she might be the first to announce the dawn of Christ's glorious Resurrection. Hence Cyril says on John xx. 17: *Woman who formerly was the minister of death, is the first to see and proclaim the adorable mystery of the Resurrection: thus womankind has procured absolution from ignominy, and removal of the curse.* Hereby, moreover, it is shown, so far as the state of glory is concerned, that the female sex shall suffer no hurt; but if women burn with greater charity, they shall also attain greater glory from the Divine vision: because the women whose love for our Lord was more persistent,—so much so that *when even the disciples withdrew* from the sepulchre *they did not depart,* (St. Gregory)— were the first to see Him rising in glory."

Gnosticism only through the androgynous ideal of a higher unity, in which the distinctive reality of masculinity and femininity is dissolved.[95]

From an understanding of creation theology results the concept of the essential goodness of man as male and as female. This becomes clear, last but not least, in the fact that a human being will rise to eternal life either in his masculinity or in her femininity.[96] According to this explanation, the *status subjectionis* existed before the Fall, too; however it did not mean the dominion of the one *over* the other. Rather, on account of man's social nature, the service of leadership (as dominion *for*) is necessary, whereby in marriage and in the family the husband guides the members of the family for their welfare and salvation. In marriage the wife by no means gives up her free will.[97] Instead, marriage is the setting for the highest form of friendship that is possible between human beings.[98]

Toward an understanding of the ministerial priesthood in Aquinas

After these preliminary hermeneutic considerations, let us turn to the statements of St. Thomas about the priesthood. In his early work, the *Commentary on the Sentences* [of Peter Lombard], he emphasizes that the priest is not the ruler of the Church, because in the Church there simply cannot be an order that would terminate the freedom of Christians by setting certain individuals over others. For Thomas one

[95] Cf. Klauck, *Religiöse Umwelt,* p. 188.

[96] Cf. SCG 4, 83: In eternal life the defects of the body will be gone. Being of the female sex remains, because it is not a defect, but rather belongs to the integrity of human nature and of the female body.

[97] Cf. ST 1, 96, 4.

[98] SCG 3, 123; *maxima amicitia.*

thing is certain: the Church in a given age may not be able to avoid the surrounding social and cultural influences, but neither can she allow her sacramental structure to be replaced by a contemporary societal order (feudal society, absolute monarchy). The Church is and remains sacramental, and the theologians of the Middle Ages describe her, with the help of biblical terms, in her relation to Christ as "(mystical) Body", as "Bride" or as "Christ's flock".

Nevertheless, based on the sacramental nature of the Church, there is a certain order placing some individual members of Christ's Body ahead of others through priestly ordination. The priests are not ordained for their own sake, however, but so that they may seek the salvation of others in the name of Christ and with his authority; Christ after all, by laying down his life, did not subject the Church to himself as an object of exploitation and domination, but rather in love obtained the salvation of believers and restored to them their liberty, freed from sin and surpassing all expectations. A man receives priestly ordination so as to represent, in his person, Christ's ongoing influence upon the Church, in the Holy Spirit, and to bring this about spiritually as well, by virtue of the authority he has bestowed. "The ministers of the Church are placed over others, not to confer anything on them by virtue of their own holiness (for this belongs to God alone), but as ministers, and as instruments, so to say, of the outpouring from the Head to the members."[99]

Citing Augustine,[100] he emphasizes that the man who is placed before others (*prae-latus*) in the Church is not somebody who is set over others and promoted in that sense. His preeminence consists of being there *for* the others. The

[99] *Suppl.* 36, 3 ad 2; 37, 4.
[100] *Civitas Dei* 19, 19.

prae-esse is rooted in the *prod-esse*:[101] "Thus a man may know himself to be no bishop if he loves to precede rather than to profit others."[102]

The Scholastic question about the recipient of the Sacrament of Orders

Scholastic theologians posed the question about whether the female sex was not just a canonical but also a dogmatic impediment to Orders. In his reply Thomas first notes, quite traditionally, that women were prophetesses—an even higher charism compared with the priesthood, though not a ministry; that women are no different from a man with respect to their soul, which is the basis of a personal relationship with God and with one's fellow men; that in the ecclesiastical realm women assume responsibility as superiors of women's religious communities and in the secular realm even exercise civil authority as rulers.

Furthermore Thomas—again within the exegetical tradition of interpreting the biblical prohibition against women teaching—distinguishes "private" teaching (catechesis, especially at home and in the family, today surely in school as well) and prophetic speech, which befits women too (and laymen in general), from the "public" teaching ministry of the Church, i.e., the authoritative, almost sacramental "proclamation of the Gospel and of the Church's doctrine", which is the province only of the bishops and priests who

[101] ST 2-2, 184, 6.
[102] ST 2-2, 185, 1 ad 1. Cf. Walter Kasper, "Steuermann mitten im Sturm: Das Bischofsamt nach Thomas von Aquin", in idem, *Theologie und Kirche,* vol. 2 (Mainz, 1999), pp. 103–27. Ulrich Horst, *Bishöfe und Ordensleute.* Cura principalis animarum *und* via perfectionis *in der Ekklesiologie des hl. Thomas von Aquin* (Berlin, 1999).

are entrusted with this ministry in virtue of the Sacrament of Orders.[103]

Thomas declares that a woman does not receive priestly ordination with respect to its substance (*res sacramenti*), even if the external ceremonies of consecration (*sacramentum tantum*) are carried out; this is true not only *de necessitate praecepti* but also *de necessitate sacramenti* [i.e., it would be neither a licit nor a valid ordination]; in making this declaration, he appeals to Christ's institutional will, which is manifested in the Church's practice.[104] Thomas does not proceed anthropologically from a *lex naturalis* to draw conclusions about divine law; rather he starts with the *ius divinum*, which is positively anchored in Christ's institutional will, and tries to make it more plausible through anthropological considerations (*lege naturali*). Therefore his teaching is not based on arguments of suitability, but rather upon the *ius divinum*,

---

[103] ST 2–2, 177, 2.

[104] *Suppl.* 39, 1 corp.: "Etsi mulieri exhibeantur omnia quae in ordinibus fiunt, ordinem non suscipit." Even though, according to the present state of historical-critical exegesis, the classical scriptural argument from the prohibition of public teaching and of ruling over one's husband (1 Tim 2:12; 1 Cor 14:34; 1 Cor 11:6) cannot be taken without further elucidation as the expression of Jesus' institutional will for the priesthood, Thomas' argumentation cannot simply be dismissed as the result of his private exegesis. For he is expressing here the universal belief and the doctrinal consensus of the Church. The dogmatic teaching of the Church developed as a reflection upon her practice, which went back to the apostolic age and the early Church, and not from an exegesis of biblical texts, which were supposed to help answer the question —at a considerable remove in time and subject matter—whether the existing practice should be continued or a new one should be introduced. In considering the question of whether the prohibition against public teaching justifies the impossibility of [women's] ordination, many critics overlook the fact that the mission to apostolic teaching, being a *ministry of the Word*, represents for the ancient Church an integral, if not entirely systematic, approach to determining the nature of the ordained priesthood.

which he takes from Scripture, tradition, and the Church's doctrine.

Using terms from sacramental theology, Thomas refers to the *sign* of a certain degree of preeminence [German—*Vorrang*; Latin—*praeesse*] that is required for the valid reception of the sacrament. Thomas does not derive this sign clearly enough from the positive, predetermined character of the relation between man and woman or from a more precise description of the man's natural aptitude for representing Christ. He limits himself to a reference to the woman's *status subjectionis* as the reason why she cannot receive Holy Orders.

Some reasons of suitability given by Aquinas

There is no detailed explanation in this context. Only a glance at his teaching about creation and at his anthropology (from the later period) brings us a little farther.[105] When Thomas explains the difference between man and woman, with regard to the individual human being as well, as a kind of descent (citing the notion about the development of male and female individuals that was usual in the natural philosophy of the day), this does not contradict the truth of creation theology, that man and woman—in their distinctiveness, personal independence, and relatedness—correspond to God's plan and show forth the beauty of creation.

A slavish subordination (*subjectio servilis*) of subjects to rulers, of women to men, whereby the latter subjugate and exploit the former, originates in sin and contradicts the freedom for which Christ has set us free (Gal 5:1), their equality with one another, and also their unity with Christ by virtue of Baptism (Gal 3:28).

[105] ST 1, 92.

In contrast, there is in every natural society (first of all in the family) a *subjectio oeconomica*, that is, a natural subordination of the one to the other, even before the fall of our first parents. Every society needs the leadership of the wise in order to direct the multiplicity of its members toward the common goal and the welfare of the individual. Thomas ascribes this preeminence in the gift of leadership on principle (if not exclusively) more to the man, since he possesses a greater *discretio rationis*. In any case, in Thomas we do not find a "subjugation" of women to men in the sense that the Romans "subjugated" Judaea to their rule.

This speculative justification that Thomas offers for the invalidity of ordination conferred upon women is unsatisfactory, to be sure. In any case, the fact remains that for Thomas, too, the *real reason* that Holy Orders is reserved for men consists positively in the institution of the sacrament by Christ, which results in the symbolic relation of Christ to the Church, which is represented by the priest. He must be a man for the sake of this symbolism, in which he is the head of a wife, just as Christ is the Head of the Church (Eph 5:23), and he portrays, symbolically and really, the relation of Christ to the Church, which is the source of his salvific action: "as Christ loved the church and gave himself up for her" (Eph 5:25).

Therefore the priest—who as servant of Christ carries on Christ's saving mission in the proclamation of the Word and in the sacraments and builds up the Church as the Body of Christ—must be conformed in his humanity to Christ, the Head, just as an instrument must be in a suitable proportion to the one who uses it.[106]

In the Incarnation Christ assumed the human nature com-

---

[106] SCG, 4, 74.

mon to all, specified by the male sex, yet born as God-Man from a woman alone, in order to indicate the salvation that encompasses both sexes and to reveal this salvation in his stance vis-à-vis the Church (as his Bride, his Body), in the relation of Bridegroom to Bride.[107]

Some Christians receive priestly ordination and function in the person of the Head, which is Christ—not so as to symbolize some natural superiority of men over women or so as to be lifted up to Christ's level. Inasmuch as grace flows out from Christ upon the Church, he alone is the Head and Shepherd of his Church. The external government of the Church is entrusted to the bishops, because they represent Christ as the basis for the unity in variety of the many members of the Church. They act as proxies of Christ and thus symbolize, in the visible realm of ecclesiastical life, the original relation of Christ, the Head and the Shepherd, to his Church.[108]

3.8 The unanimous belief of the Church in the modern era until the debate about women's ordination after Vatican II

For the period of post-Tridentine theology, which extends well into the nineteenth century, we find an uncontested unanimity of all the authoritative theologians, an agreement that the teaching about the connection between Holy Orders and the male sex is of divine right and proceeds necessarily from the nature of the Sacrament of Orders as a representation of Christ.[109] Accordingly any eventual conferral of ordination upon women is considered invalid. Some hold the opinion that the Church could confer minor orders upon

[107] ST 3, 31, 4; *Suppl.* 36, 2.
[108] ST 3, 8, 6; Augustine, *In Evang. Johan.*, PL 35, 1750.
[109] Ott, *Weihesakrament*, pp. 165f.

women. In their speculations, most authors cite the societal subordination of women as the justification for their non-admission to Orders. Already in the Middle Ages, though, critics of this argument appeared. Following them, Honoré de Tournely,[110] for example, traces the reservation of Holy Orders to male recipients back to a positive command and expressly rejects an innate incapacity of a woman to receive the Sacrament of Orders. The argument must be made from the institutional will of Christ and from the nature of the sacrament, not from aspects of womanly existence that "exclude" woman from the priesthood.

In the twentieth century and in the magisterial documents that have proliferated since the 1960s, this speculative argument (the *subjectio oeconomica*) disappears completely and is even explicitly rejected. The Magisterium maintains the unanimous practice, though, because it is convinced that the arguments adduced by way of explanation were not the actual, material reason for the faith conviction that the Church can validly administer this sacrament only to a baptized man.

Of course the classical argument is not simply being replaced. Based on the distinction between positive and speculative theology, the actual and normative validity of the practice—as it has come to light in Scripture and tradition, as well as in binding doctrinal pronouncements—becomes the starting point for a new reflection upon the real foundation that lies in the nature of the Sacrament of Orders. The more recent argumentation, even in its speculative justification for the practice, remains aligned with the principal tradition of sacramental theology, in that the argument cites the representation of Christ[111] as Head of the Church, who

---

[110] *Praelectiones theologicae* (1729) 10, 5, 1755.
[111] Paul Josef Cordes, " 'Sacerdos alter Christus'? Der Repräsentations-

reveals himself in signs as the cause of salvation with respect to the Church through the "fundamental symbolism of the man-woman relationship".[112]

4. Conclusion

The practice of the Catholic Church, from the early Church to the present, of conferring the Sacrament of Holy Orders

---

gedanke in der Amtstheologie", *Cath* 26 (1972): 38–49; idem, *Sendung zum Dienst: Exegetisch-historische und systematische Studien zum Konzilsdekret "Vom Dienst und Leben der Priester"*, FThS, 9 (Frankfurt, 1972); Leo Scheff-czyk, "Die Christusrepräsentation als Wesensmoment des Priester-amtes", in idem, *Schwerpunkte des Glaubens,* Horizonte NF, 11 (Einsiedeln, 1977), pp. 367–86; Gisbert Greshake, article "Priester/Priestertum III.2. Systematisch", in TRE 27 (1977): 422–31.

[112] More and more often since around 1970, doubt has been expressed, by Catholic theologians as well, about the relevance of unanimous [his-torical] practice for what is [to be considered] binding in faith, with regard to the constitutive aspects of the Sacrament of Orders. The opin-ion that these doubts can drive the explicit declarations of the Church's Magisterium in recent times back to the level of a private opinion, thus leaving the decision ultimately to the trend in opinions, can scarcely be reconciled with the Catholic interpretation of doctrine. Vincent of Lérins, *Commonitorium* 2, cites universality, antiquity, and consensus as the criteria for what can be called Catholic: "We shall follow universal-ity if we profess as the one true faith the faith that is professed by the whole Church throughout the world; [we shall follow] the antiquity [of an article of faith] if we in no way depart from the doctrines that our holy predecessors and fathers [of the Church] manifestly proclaimed; [we shall follow] the consensus also if we adhere to the decisions and statements [*definitiones sententiasque*] of all or almost all bishops [*sacerdotes*] and teachers within that same antiquity." [Translated into English from Latin with reference to the German. Cf. Rouët de Journel, *Enchiridion Patristicum,* no. 2168.] Cf. also *Commonitorium* 27, and DV 10: "But the task of giving an authentic interpretation of the Word of God, whether in its written form or in the form of Tradition, has been entrusted to the living teaching office of the Church alone. Its authority in this matter is exercised in the name of Jesus Christ."

only upon baptized men who are in full communion with it, is unanimous.

It is rooted in the belief that, according to the institutional will of Christ (with regard to the company of disciples and the Church, to the apostolate and the Sacrament of Orders), only a man can receive this sacrament validly, not because of a superiority of men over women, but because the Sacrament of Orders presupposes the natural symbolism of the relation between husband and wife. The difference between man and woman does not result in any anthropological deficiency, but is rather the prerequisite for the full realization of *being human in communion*; it follows that nontransferable characteristics of masculinity or femininity do not constitute a restriction of the possibilities of one sex by the other. The opposite is the case:

The contrast between man and woman, from which results the creaturely existence of humanity in nature, in history, and in society, is precisely what makes it possible to give oneself, indeed to give *one's self* to another and to convey ownership of oneself to him. A woman is not deprived of the human possibility of being masculine or "excluded" from the possibility of becoming a father. Neither is a man, naturally speaking, excluded from motherhood or, with respect to the history of salvation (Gal 4:4), "excluded" from the Divine Motherhood because the Incarnation and thus the theandric *communio* of love took place through the sole and unique cooperation of a woman (cf. Gal 4:4–6; Rom 8:15; Jn 1:14; 2:2; 1 Jn 1:1–3; 4:8, 12).

Being a priest is not an occupation or a societal position or role, any more than being a father or a mother is. Priesthood denotes a personal relation, or better, the representation of one person by another. Jesus Christ, according to the unanimous witnesses to the Church's faith, is symbolically represented by a baptized man by virtue of the Sacrament of Holy Orders. This representation of Christ pertains (and is restricted) to his paternal and foundational relationship to the Church as her Bridegroom/Head. Other modes of representing Christ are thus not excluded but rather brought to light.

If a woman cannot symbolically represent Jesus Christ, the Son of the Eternal Father, in this sense as Bridegroom/Head of the Church—just as, conversely, the man cannot represent the (bridal) relationship of the Church to Christ —that does not mean that she is, so to speak, "excluded" or "barred" from the priesthood. The reason is that she, through the feminine mode of her humanity, represents the Church in her communion with Christ and thus also represents, to the world and to her fellow believers in the Church, "Christ united with the Church as one Person". The Church receives this union with Christ through God's self-communication, and she makes it visible sacramentally in faith and love in service to neighbor for his spiritual salvation and physical well-being.

Ecclesial life is not exhausted in the activity of the priest; rather, God appointed "pastors and teachers, for the equipment of [i.e., in order to equip] the saints for the work of ministry, for building up the body of Christ" (Eph 4:11–12). Therefore the members of Christ's Body who do not exercise an apostolic-priestly ministry, the "laity" (men and women), are not relegated to second-class membership or condemned to passivity.

When Christ chose men to be his apostles and thus established the norm for the Church's selection of ordained ministers, it was not a merely arbitrary decision. The positive justification of this decision ought to be understood, rather, on the basis of its own significance and content, and it must be explained in terms of the fundamental structure of the order of creation and redemption.

If in the life of the contemporary Church the priest is viewed again in a stronger sacramental-theological light, and the Church herself is seen less functionally and more theologically, then it may become plausible again to many people why the specific relation of Christ as Head to the Church as his Body and his Bride is represented in the primordial symbol of the man-woman correlative.

Just as only a man, a husband, can become a father through his self-giving love for his wife, while his wife by conception and birth presents him with a child, in whom the love of them both has become "flesh", so too only the priest *can* —inasmuch as a reference to woman is indicated in his masculinity—sacramentally symbolize the relation of Christ as Bridegroom and Head of his Church.

> Sent as he is by the Father to govern his family, a bishop should keep before his eyes the example of the Good Shepherd. . . . The priests, prudent cooperators of the episcopal college. . ., called to the service of the People of God, constitute, together with their bishop, a unique sacerdotal college (*presbyterium*). . . . They (the priests) should bestow their paternal attention and solicitude on [the faithful], whom they have begotten spiritually through baptism and instruction (cf. 1 Cor 4:15; 1 Pet 1:23). (LG 27–28)

Since it is not only a question of a formal opposition [*Gegenüber*], but also of a personal, relational encounter [*Gegenüber*] of Christ and the Church, the recipient of the Sacrament of Holy Orders cannot simply be "just" (abstractly) a human person endowed with spiritual authority. He must be a person, a soul-body composite, who by participating in a relational symbolism [i.e., sexual complementarity] typologically and thus sacramentally makes visible the specific opposition of Christ to the Church as Bridegroom to Bride.

Vatican II explained more precisely the nature of the ministerial priesthood as follows:

> By the sacrament of Order priests are configured to Christ the priest as servants of the Head, so that as co-workers with the episcopal order they may build up the Body of Christ, the Church. . . . They are consecrated to God in a new way in their ordination and are made the living instruments of Christ the eternal priest, and so are enabled to accomplish throughout all time that wonderful work of his which with supernatural efficacy restored the whole human race. Since every priest in his own way assumes the person of Christ he is endowed with a special grace. By this grace the priest, through his service of the people committed to his care and all the People of God, is able the better to pursue the perfection of Christ, whose place he takes. (PO 12)

And referring directly to the correlation between Christ as Head and Christ as Body, the Council declares:

> Priests exercise the function of Christ as Pastor and Head in proportion to their share of authority. In the name of the bishop they gather the family of God as a brotherhood endowed with the spirit of unity and lead it in Christ through the Spirit to God the Father. (PO 6; LG 28)

IV

THE SACRAMENTAL DIACONATE

1. Its origin in the *diakonia* of Jesus Christ

With the Incarnation of the Word that is God and through which the world came into being (Jn 1:1–18), the greatest revolution imaginable was accomplished in mankind.

In the history of religion until then there had been a clear separation between the "gods above" and the "men as their servants below", and social and political power structures were marked by the sharp distinction between rulers and subjects, masters and slaves; now, however, God, the Creator of heaven and earth, has made himself the servant of men in his consubstantial Son, who has appeared in lowly form among men in the "likeness of . . . flesh" (Rom 8:3).

1.1 *Christ as Deacon*

The *Kyrios* of all men is the *diakonos* of all. God, the Lord, encounters us in God the Servant. Jesus Christ, the Father's own Son (Rom 1:3), who was in the *morphe theou* [the form of God, cf. Phil 2:6], did not hold his equality with God in his grasp, the way a thief or a predatory animal clutches what it has snatched. No: "[He] emptied himself, taking the form of a servant [*morphe doulou*], being born in the likeness of men. And being found in human form he humbled himself and became obedient unto death, even death on a cross" (Phil 2:7f.).

183

As the *doulos* who obediently carries out the salvific will of the Father, Jesus Christ has been established as the Lord of all creation—to the glory of God the Father, to whom he will restore the divine rule at the end of time by subjecting himself to him (1 Cor 15:28). Through him God exercises his dominion by destroying the powers of darkness, sin, and death, which rob man of his freedom and his life (Rom 8:38f.).

In obedience to his Father, therefore, Jesus brought about the divine rule by virtue of his messianic activity and destiny, not with a display of imperial power, courtroom rhetoric, intellectual superiority, political cunning, or dazzling self-promotion, but rather in the utmost submission of his life: "For the Son of man also came not to be served but to serve, and to give his life as a ransom for many" (Mk 10:45).

The victory of God's wisdom over human wisdom through the foolishness and weakness of Christ's Cross (1 Cor 1:23f.) could hardly be presented more impressively than in the account of the foot-washing in the upper room at the Last Supper. The Evangelist states the motive of this incomparable symbolic action of Jesus: "[H]aving loved his own who were in the world, he loved them to the end" (Jn 13:1).

And Jesus himself explains the meaning of the foot-washing. The disciples are right to call him their *Didaskolos* and *Kyrios*. But he has performed for them this service, like a slave, in order to give them an example, so that they too will serve one another, as their Lord and Teacher has served them (Jn 13:13–15). Christ's purpose in liberating mankind from slavery to sin and overcoming alienation from God was not to enable the oppressed to pay back their former masters or to view their liberation merely as the formal equality of all before the law. Nor is it a matter of everyone receiving a share of the "power", as is the case in the civil realm at the transition from an absolute monarchy to a constitutional one, or from a dictatorship to a democracy.

Jesus Christ, rather, has brought about man's freedom from himself—so profoundly and radically, in fact, that men realize their potential by the very fact that they freely have the opportunity to make themselves servants of salvation for others. They live on the basis of Jesus' dedication [*Pro-Existenz*, from Latin *prodesse*] and re-present it in their own availability for others. The one who pursues happiness in life by all means does not deserve to be called a disciple of Jesus; rather, the one who "loses his life for [Jesus'] sake and the gospel's will save it" (Mk 8:35). What characterizes the disciple of Jesus is not that he exercises power over others for his own advantage, but rather that he receives from Jesus the power to make himself available as a servant in spreading the reign of God.

For this reason Jesus had appointed the Twelve, "to be with him, and to be sent out to preach and have authority to cast out demons" (Mk 3:14f.). Yet this service in the Kingdom of God is not intended as a means of increasing one's personal power or prestige, of having a brilliant career, of satisfying ambitions, or realizing one's potential in an impressive position, or of enjoying the so-called security of the lifetime appointee or the millions earned by sports stars and CEOs. In radical contrast to the rulers and the powerful of this world, who abuse their power by oppressing and exploiting men, the first among the disciples shall be the one who is willing to become the *diakonos* and *doulos* of all (Mk 10:43).

From this christological perspective results an essential characteristic of being a Christian. Christian existence is a participation in the *diakonia* that God himself performed for mankind in Christ, and so it is an indication of what it means for man to be fulfilled and perfected. To be a Christian is to follow Christ through obedience and readiness to serve —even to the point of losing and sacrificing oneself—and thus to gain oneself in the life of charity.

Diakonein [to serve] is the lot of every Christian on the basis of his Baptism, since by virtue of his participation in the Church's *diakonia, leiturgia,* and *martyria* [service, worship, and witness] he shares the burden of Christ's service for the salvation of mankind. For as members of the Body of Christ, all should become servants of one another with the charisms that they have received for the upbuilding of the Church, the edification of their fellow Christians in faith and love: "[W]hoever renders service, [let him do so] as one who renders it by the strength which God supplies" (1 Pet 4:11; cf. Rom 12:8; 1 Cor 12:5).

This can also be accomplished concretely in particular forms of love of neighbor and of service to those who are sick (whether in body or in spirit), needy or imprisoned (Mt 25), in material relief offered for the congregations (Rom 15:25; 1 Tim 5:3–16), or in many forms of assistance and collaboration with the apostles, as we can conclude from a list of greetings to the men and women who collaborated with the Apostle Paul (Rom 16:3ff.; Phil 4:3).

1.2 *The apostolic ministry as a representation of Christ's* diakonia *to the Church*

"Service", however, is also the essential and definitive characteristic of the apostolic ministry, which gave rise to and finds its specific expression in the threefold *sacramentum ordinis;* the distinct degrees of ministry conferred in this sacrament have been designated "even from ancient times" (LG 28) by the terms *bishop*, *presbyter*, and *deacon*.[1]

The apostles are described as "God's fellow workers" and "servants" (1 Thess 3:2; 1 Cor 3:9; 2 Cor 6:1), "servants of Christ and stewards of the mysteries of God" (1 Cor 4:1). They are "ministers of the new covenant" (cf. 2 Cor 3:6) and ministers of the gospel (Col 1:23; Eph 3:6), devoting themselves to the "ministry of the word" (Acts 6:4). In their apostolic office they are "ministers of the Church", so that the word of Christ might dwell in its fullness within the faithful (Col 1:25), and thereby the Church as the Body of Christ might be built up in charity (Eph 4:12). The apostles prove themselves to be the servants of the faithful for Jesus' sake when they preach, not themselves, but Jesus Christ as Lord (2 Cor 4:5). They are men sent in place of Christ, since the word of Christ is entrusted to them to be proclaimed in the service of reconciliation. Through them, God himself *speaks* and *acts* in the Holy Spirit—the same God who has reconciled the world to himself in Jesus Christ (2 Cor 5:20).

Diakonein has proved to be a far-reaching determinant of *Christian life* at many levels: the level of (1) the sacramental foundations for being a Christian, of (2) the *charismatic* structure of the Church, as well as of (3) the mission of the apostles and of (4) the *ministerial office* of teaching, sanctifying, and governing, which has proceeded from the *apostolate*. Above and beyond this, *diakonein*, even since the

[1] Cf. Alfons Weiser, Eva-Maria Faber, Gerhard Ludwig Müller, Gisbert Greshake, article "Diakon", in *Lexikon für Theologie und Kirche*, 3d ed., 3:178–84 (Lit.). Gerhard Ludwig Müller, "Theologische Überlegungen zur Weiterentwicklung des Diakonats", MThZ 40 (1989): 129–43. Peter Hünermann et al., eds., *Ein Amt für Frauen in der Kirche— ein frauengerechtes Amt?* (Ostfildern, 1997) (Lit.).

beginning of the Church, has become a term designating a
specific ministry, namely, that of the diakonos, who acts together
with the bishops and presbyters for the Church, in the fullness of Christ's power.

2. Origin and development of the diaconal ministry

Of course the New Testament writings and the testimonies
of the Apostolic Fathers are an insufficient basis for a detailed
historical reconstruction of the beginnings of the threefold
Order, in the way unanimously professed by the Catholic
Church of the East and the West, that is, as an arrangement
of divine law that is *binding in faith*. An interpretation of
this development as a sociologically conditioned process of
specialization would contradict the epistemological criteria
and ecclesiological declarations of the Catholic faith.

2.1 *Toward a theological hermeneutic of Church*
history and of the pertinent documents

The documents show that the early Church attributes the
development of these ministries to the working of the Spirit
of God (1 Cor 12:28; Eph 4:11; Acts 20:28) and to the initiative of the apostles themselves; they owe their mission
to the Lord, who lived on earth and is now glorified, and
they saw their leading role in the Church as something established through the full authority given to them by the
Lord, while on earth and now in glory (Mk 3:13–19; 6:6–
13; Mt 28:16–20; Acts 1:15–26; Gal 1:10–24).

As a contribution to a theological interpretation of the
historical-empirical processes, we should make the following brief remarks. A hermeneutic that is determined by a
positivistic world view cannot do justice to the source ma-

terials and the actual historical development, because in principle it ignores the essence of the Church and of her institutions, which can only be explained theologically. A dualistic conception of reality brings us no farther along—the notion that the human mind moves on two completely separate and incommunicable planes, the one being a neutral ascertaining of facts and the other merely a subjective interpretation of them. From where is understanding supposed to obtain its categories and the raw materials for interpretation if not from reality, which impresses itself upon the understanding and therefore expresses within it as well its own intelligible forms, by which it is recognized by human reason?

Reason, i.e., the power of human insight, insofar as it operates in the science of theology as well, is in and of itself nothing other than the original unity between receptivity to phenomena mediated by the senses and the discovery of their supraempirical, transcendent ground of meaning. Man as a soul-body composite, a being that is both historical and transcendent, is thus also the suitable recipient of a self-revelation by God in his WORD, which became flesh, and in his SPIRIT, which as *pneuma* and *dynamis* [life-breath and power] enables man to form judgments identifying historical phenomena with the God who reveals himself through words and signs.

An historical revelation, from which the Church has proceeded and always proceeds as the People of God, the Body of Christ and the Temple of the Holy Spirit, can be interpreted only by a hermeneutic with the acuity, depth, and panoramic scope of reason illuminated by the Holy Spirit, which we call faith. Only a historical-transcendental hermeneutic is in a position to perceive, in empirically, historically observable events and the reflexive understanding of them in the faith-consciousness of the Church, the realization of the supraempirical, transcendent salvific action of God. By the very fact that God reveals himself to this faith community by his Word and his Spirit, he constitutes the Church as the witness community proceeding from this revelation and adequately representing it. Thus the reflexive understanding of the Church in the act of faith and the expression of her faith in creed and dogma are both substantiated in the revelation event itself, and not at all in subjective things-to-be-interpreted that are projected upon some thematic surface completely foreign to them. Dogma is the linguistic form assumed by the Word as a result of God's will to communicate himself—that same Word which, in the Church's verbal profession of faith, is God and has become flesh.

From this perspective of a fundamental hermeneutic of a revelation communicating itself through Word and event, theological findings can result from research into the historical testimonies about the life of the early Church.

2.2 A particular helping ministry develops from the apostolate

In the Pauline communities, besides the Apostle Paul and his fellow apostles Peter and the Twelve (1 Cor 15:3–5; Gal 2), together with these apostles and following after them, Paul's immediate coworkers in the apostolate also appear (e.g., Silvanus, Timothy, Titus, Apollos), as well as a series of people who help in the apostolic work and serve in the local communities (2 Cor 8:23), for instance Epaphroditus (Phil 2:25), Epaphras (Col 4:12), and Archippus (Col 4:17), who are called servants of Christ.

In the introduction to the letter that he wrote around the year A.D. 50 to the church at Philippi, with which the

Apostle had particularly close ties, Paul specifically greets the *episkopoi* and the *diakonoi*. Here we should already be thinking of the developing ministries related to the concrete local church. Of course no definite nomenclature exists yet for the offices of those who are "set over" others (*proistamenoi*) in the Lord, who labor and are entitled to esteem and love because of their work (1 Thess 5:12): the servants of the Church (1 Cor 16:16) and the leaders (*hegoumenoi*) to whom the congregations should be submissive (Heb 13:7, 17, 24; 1 Clement 1:3; 21:6), the "leading men" [among the brethren] (Acts 15:22) and those who rule (Rom 12:8 [Gk., Vulg., Douay-Rheims]), the apostles, prophets, and teachers (1 Cor 12:18; Gal 6:6; Acts 13:1; 4:14), the "evangelists, . . . pastors and teachers" (Eph 4:11).

The activity addressed in such terminology already points toward the ministerial titles that would become crystallized a short time later. Paul says of Stephanas, Fortunatus, and Achaicus, the first converts from Achaia, that they, together with their fellow workers and laborers, have devoted themselves to the service of the saints. The congregation should be subject to them. The command is issued to the faithful: "Give recognition to such men" (1 Cor 16:18).

The fact that different ministries are designated by the terms *episkopoi* ["overseers"] and "leaders", on the one hand, and *diakonoi*, on the other, is evident from descriptions of their different functions (cf. 1 Tim 3:8–13; *Constitutio apostolorum* 8, 46).

Incidentally, several things should be noted briefly about linguistic usage and, more importantly, about the theological content of the episcopal and presbyteral ministries.

Episkopos should by no means be understood, based on the use of the term in secular Greek sources, as a merely political or statutory administrative and supervisory office in the community. Linguistic usage in the New Testament essentially bears the stamp of the Greek in the Septuagint, in which God appears as the Shepherd and *Episkopos* of Israel, who looks into man's soul and protects him (Job 20:29 [LXX]; Wis 1:6). Hence the fact that the head of the Christian community (of presbyters, i.e., the class of those appointed to spiritual ministry) and of the servants of the Word who preach and teach (1 Tim 5:17; 1 Clement 44:5; 47:6; 54:2; 57:1) is termed the *episkopos* (1 Tim 3:2; Tit 1:5; Acts 20:28; 1 Pet 5:1–4; 1 Clement 42–44) must also be explained in the sense of a pastoral (shepherding) and leadership function. This is true because the presbyters, who pasture God's flock *episcopaliter* [in the manner of bishops] in union with the Apostle Peter, who describes himself as their fellow presbyter (1 Pet 5:1), will receive their reward from the Chief Shepherd, namely, from Christ, "the Shepherd and Guardian [*Episkopos*] of your souls" (1 Pet 2:25). Jesus, the Good Shepherd, who lays down his life for his sheep (Jn 10:11), is the archetype and model for the pastoral ministry of the apostles (Jn 21:15–19), who, by virtue of the Holy Spirit whom they have received, continue Christ's salvific mission from the Father (Jn 20:22f.). The *episkope* that the Apostle Matthias took over in the place of Judas (Acts 1:20, 25–26) can hardly have been an external supervisory office;[2] rather, it was understood as a pastoral ministry, which was later handed on to the church leaders as well. Paul, speaking to the presbyters of the Church of Ephesus (Acts 20:17), said "Take heed to yourselves and to all the flock, in which the Holy Spirit has made you guardians [*episkópous*], to feed

---

[2] The Greek work *episkopé* (Acts 1:20 = Ps 69:26 LXX) is not adequately rendered by the term "ministry" (*Amt*, in the *Einheitsübersetzung*, the German Church Unity translation of the Bible). Luther translated it as *Bistum* (= "episcopacy", precisely the office of the bishop).

the church of the Lord which he obtained with his own blood" (Acts 20:28).

It is well known that our English word *priest*, too [cf. Ger. *Priester*, Fr. *prêtre*], is derived from the biblical word *presbyter*, the leader of the congregation and "minister of the word" (Lk 1:2; Acts 6:4; 1 Tim 5:17). The terms *hiereus/sacerdos*, drawn from the Old Testament, with an allusion to the description of Christ as the High Priest, were not used to describe the ministry of the apostles, teachers, bishops, and presbyters until the *Didache* and the First Letter of Clement. This should not mislead us, however, to the erroneous conclusion that the offices of bishops and priests in the early Church had a profane origin and that sacred terminology was deliberately avoided. In fact the relation of Christ to the Church, to the apostles, and to the ministries that proceed from them cannot be comprehended by means of the contrast "profane/sacred", a pair of terms from the history of religions. Against the background of revelation another question entirely arises: Are these missions and duties to be understood as the workings of God, of Christ, and of the Holy Spirit, so that Christ in person, as Head of the Church, is present through the apostles; *or* do the ministries of proclaiming the gospel and building up the community, performed by pastors who are appointed by the Spirit of God (Acts 20:28), have their origin in a purely profane effort to organize the community, which only accidentally has to do with its intrinsic nature as the People of God, the Body of Christ, and the Temple of the Holy Spirit?

Neither in Sacred Scripture nor in any passage from the Church Fathers is there the faintest hint of an indication that could support the latter view.

The church leaders, who work to build up the Church as pastors and teachers of the community (Eph 4:11) in the

place of and as successors (Eph 2:20) to the apostles and early
Church prophets and teachers, were probably termed presbyters at first in the Jewish-Christian communities, while
in the pagan Christian communities they were called by the
title *episkopos*.

The *episkopoi* are always mentioned together with the *diakonoi* (Phil 1:1; 1 Tim 3:1–13; *Didache* 15:1; 1 Clement
42:5). After the apostolic, foundational period, once the local churches became clearly defined in their supraregional
communion with the *Ecclesia catholica*,[3] the threefold ministry emerges more clearly at the beginning of the second
century.

In each local church there is a college of community pastors and gospel teachers, whose president is then referred to
by the ministerial title of bishop, which is reserved to him.
To the bishop and the presbyterium is ordered a group of
ministers who are called deacons.[4]

2.3 The differentiation and definition of a degree of
Orders distinct from the episcopacy and the presbyterate

The apostolate was handed on by degrees, inasmuch as duties were divided up and certain ones were carried out in a
particular area of responsibility and took on an independent
form as a specific ministry. The meaning and necessity of
this development prove to be founded as early as the apostles' initiative of establishing, besides their ministry of the
Word in the mother Church of Jerusalem, a special *ministry*

[3] Ignatius of Antioch, *Smyrn.* 8, 2.
[4] Ignatius of Antioch, *Magn.* 2; 6, 1; 13, 1; *Trall.* 2, 2f.; 3, 1; 7, 2;
Philad., praes., 4; 7, 1; 10, 2; *Smyrn.* 8, 1; 12, 2; *Pol.* 6, 1; Polycarp of
Smyrna, 2 *Phil., praes.*

of serving tables. The selection of seven men, and their appointment to the *table ministry* through prayer and the laying on of hands by the apostles, cannot be understood simply as the institution of the diaconate as the first degree of the tripartite sacramental *Ordo*.[5] Historically it could very well have been a matter of the board of directors of the Hellenistic Christian community. One of their number, Philip, then appears as an evangelist and early Christian itinerant missionary (Acts 8). Together with the early Christian prophets and teachers (Acts 13:1-3), they probably belong to the circle of "leading men" (Acts 15:22) that we encounter, in conjunction with the apostles, under the general heading of "apostles and elders [i.e., presbyters]" (Acts 1:25; 15:2, 6, 22).

This much is clear, however: the development of a specific ministry of service to the people, particularly addressing their physical and spiritual needs, is due to the working of the Spirit in the early Church and to the initiative of the apostles. "Therefore, brethren, pick out from among you seven men of good repute, full of the Spirit and of wisdom, whom we may appoint to this duty" (Acts 6:3).

If one reflects that service to one's neighbor in need makes Christ present and mediates his saving love, indeed, that in the needy persons Christ himself is served, then the ministry of the deacon in the social and charitable sphere proves to be a mission thoroughly inspired by the Holy Spirit, a mission that creates a special personal relationship with Christ, the Head of the Church, and which therefore is specifically conferred by the laying on of hands in ordination.

Polycarp of Smyrna calls the deacons servants of God and

---

[5] Thus at least Irenaeus of Lyons, *Haer.* 1, 26, 3.

of Christ, who by virtue of their exemplary Christian way
of life devote themselves to the care of others, "*compassion-
ate, industrious*, walking according to the truth of the *Lord*,
who was the *servant (diakonos)* of all."[6]

In the pastoral letters criteria for the appointment of deacons are mentioned. Timothy has the duty of supervising
the presbyters and bishops, and he must not lay hands upon
any one of them and appoint him to his ministry without
first testing him (1 Tim 5:22); he also accepts the Apostle Paul's instruction with regard to the deacons. Not being
leaders in the Church, the latter are not immediately responsible for proclaiming Christian doctrine. But with a clear
conscience they should hold fast to the *mystery of the faith*
(1 Tim 3:9) and demonstrate by their character and by their
care for their families that they are tried and true. "[F]or
those who serve well as deacons gain a good standing for
themselves and also great confidence in the faith which is
in Christ Jesus" (1 Tim 3:13).

The ministries of bishop, presbyter, and deacon are anchored in Christ's institutional will and in the working of
the Spirit in the birth and fundamental development of the
Church, as her constitutive charisms, works, and ministries
unfolded (1 Cor 12:4–6) and also in the competence of
the apostles to shape this development (Acts 6:4; 14:23;
20:28; Eph 4:11; Tit 1:5); thus these ministries belong to
the divinely ordained essence and sacramental structure of
the Church. This insight is consolidated in the years immediately following the apostolic age.

In the *Didache* the community is admonished to select as
bishops and deacons only those men who are worthy and
have been tested, because they perform their ministry *to-*

[6] 2 Phil 5:2.

gether with the "prophets, teachers, and apostles" (cf. 1 Cor 12:28), who on account of their lofty position are the "honored members" of the community (*Didache* 15, 1–3). They have their specific responsibilities with regard to the proclamation of the Word and the Eucharist (10, 7), by analogy with the prophets, "who are your high priests" (13, 3).

Clement of Rome (around A.D. 96) was a disciple of the apostles. According to his testimony, the apostles went about preaching and founding churches; in every place where they labored they chose men from among the first converts to the faith (cf. 1 Cor 16:15) and appointed them, "having first proved them by the Spirit, to be bishops and deacons of those who should afterwards believe" (1 Clement 42, 4).

There is a certain analogy to the Old Testament ministry of the high priest, to whom the priests and the Levites were subordinated with regard to the members of the *laos tou theou*, the "laity" (1 Clement 40, 5). Thus the apostles incorporated these ministers into the mission that they, the apostles, had received from Christ (Jn 20:21), who was himself sent by the Father (1 Clement 42, 1). For their part, the bishops/presbyters are commanded to take care that after their death other "respected men" take over their ministry (44, 2f.). Paul had already commanded Timothy to see to the appointment of further teachers of the Gospel: "You then, my son, be strong in the grace that is in Christ Jesus, and what you have heard from me before many witnesses entrust to faithful men who will be able to teach others also" (2 Tim 2:1f.).

Ignatius of Antioch speaks about the deacons "of the mysteries of Jesus Christ", who as servants of God's Church must be ready to offer help to all. "Let everyone revere the deacons as Jesus Christ, the bishop as the image of the Father, and the presbyters as the senate of God and the assembly of the apostles. For without them one cannot speak of the Church."[7]

The remarkable thing about this statement is the conviction, which is central to ecclesiology and the theology of ministry, that the *one* salvific ministry of Christ, who is the sole Mediator between the one God and the many who comprise mankind (1 Tim 2:4–7), is exercised within the Church and with respect to his Church by the *one* ministry (in its various subdivisions) that has in the *bishop* the *source and foundation of its own unity and of the unity of the whole Church* (cf. LG 23). Just as important, moreover, is the conviction that, without bishop, presbytery, and deacons and unity with them, one cannot speak of the Church at all. Therefore he says, "Let all follow the bishop, as Jesus Christ follows his Father, and the college of presbyters as the apostles; respect the deacons as you do God's law."[8]

Thus the threefold ministry is no human invention. It belongs to the sacramental nature of the Church, inasmuch as the Church is the object of faith, which depends upon the working of the Holy Spirit. The invisible and the visible dimensions of the Church do not belong to two different realities; rather they constitute the essence of the one Church. Therefore we must say that the visible social form of the Church is actually a representation of her invisible essence, which is accessible only to faith.

Only in union with the bishop—an office which is unthinkable without the presbyterium and the deacons—is the Catholic Church recognizable as Christ's Church. Expressed here is an acknowledgment of [1] the divine origin of the one ministerial Order in the New Testament and its divinely

---

[7] Ignatius, *Trall.* 2, 3–3, 1.
[8] Ignatius, *Smyrn.* 8, 1f.

willed exercise in the three different degrees, [2] the ministry of unity vested in the bishop, and [3] the ministry of collegiality (multiplicity) in the assembly of the presbyters and in the subordinate range of duties belonging to the deacons of Jesus Christ.

In canon 6 of its Decree on Ordination (1563), the Council of Trent is entirely correct when it expresses the Catholic belief as follows: "If anyone says that in the Catholic Church a hierarchy has not been instituted by divine ordinance, which consists of the bishops, priests, and ministers" then he contradicts revelation and the will of God for his Church (DH 1776; 3860). The Church's belief in the divine institution of the sacramental *Ordo*, subdivided as bishop, presbyter, and deacon, is also formulated unambiguously by the Second Vatican Council.

> That divine mission, which was committed by Christ to the apostles, is destined to last until the end of the world (cf. Mt 28:20), since the Gospel, which they were charged to hand on, is, for the Church, the principle of all its life for all time. For that very reason the apostles were careful to appoint successors in this hierarchically constituted society.
>
> In fact, not only had they various helpers in their ministry, but, in order that the mission entrusted to them might be continued after their death, they consigned, by will and testament, as it were, to their immediate collaborators the duty of completing and consolidating the work they had begun. . . . In that way, then, with priests and deacons as helpers, the bishops received the charge of the community. (LG 20)

Already at the time of Ignatius, the intrinsic connections between one's understanding of the Church, the celebration of the Eucharist, and the missionary duty of the bishop were an important part of the Church's faith. Only the bishop, and the presbyter whom he has authorized, presides at the celebration of the Eucharist. The deacon, however, can assist the bishop in the proclamation of the Word.[9]

The various duties [1] of the ministry of unity, which are incumbent upon the bishop, [2] of the pastoral leadership of the congregation by the presbyters who preside, and [3] of the deacons, who "are entrusted with the ministry of Jesus Christ",[10] receive their fullest, most concentrated expression in the celebration of the Eucharist, as the fundamental sacramental act of the Church. "Take care, then, to partake of one Eucharist; for, one is the Flesh of our Lord Jesus Christ, and one the cup to unite us with his Blood, and one altar, just as there is one bishop assisted by the presbytery and the deacons, my fellow servants. Thus you will conform in all your actions to the will of God." So writes Ignatius to the Philadelphians.[11]

In the middle of the second century, Justin the philosopher describes the duty of the deacon at the eucharistic celebration. After the Eucharistic Prayer of the presider (*proestotos*), that is, the bishop or the presbyter, the deacons distribute the consecrated gifts to the faithful who are present and bring them also to those who are absent.[12]

Deacons assist in administering Baptism (*Traditio apostolica* 21). In emergencies they themselves may baptize, as the Council of Elvira testifies (306/309).[13] It is added, however, that a supplementary laying on of hands by the bishop is

---

[9] Ignatius, *Trall.* 2, 3: "[The deacons] are not mere dispensers of meat and drink, but servants of the Church of God", and Ignatius, *Philad.* 11, 1: "Philo, the deacon from Cilicia who has been so well spoken of, is at present giving me his help in preaching God's word."

[10] Ignatius, *Magn.* 6, 1.

[11] Ignatius, *Philad.* 4.

[12] Justin, *1 Apol.* 65; 67. Cf. Hippolytus, *Trad. apost.* 4; 21; 22. Cyprian, *De lapsis* 25.

[13] Can. 77; DH 121.

necessary, after the example of the apostles, who laid hands upon the faithful of Samaria baptized by the "deacon" Philip, so as to confer the Holy Spirit upon them (cf. Acts 8:14ff.).

In danger of death, or when the bishop or presbyter cannot be reached, the deacons are even allowed to impose hands upon penitents for their reconciliation.[14] This, however, is not to be understood as priestly absolution (as in later custom of private Confession), since in the early Church the power of expiating sins was attributed to the penitential works, and this power took on a concrete ecclesiological form in the ceremony of reconciliation determined by the bishop.

The charitable works of the deacon with respect to the widows and orphans, the poor and the needy, are often spoken of in the early Church.[15] Deacons are mentioned as administrators of Church property.[16]

In the *Traditio apostolica* Hippolytus gives a glimpse of the liturgy and theology of ordination at the turn of the third century. In marked contrast to the various nonsacramental ecclesial offices that have come into being meanwhile, he speaks of the bishop, the presbyter, and the deacon, who are consecrated and empowered to perform their duties through the laying on of hands by the bishop, which equips them with the Holy Spirit.

The deacon does not become a *sacerdos* (which denotes the bishop and the presbyter), but is ordained to serve the bishop, in a ceremony whereby the latter only imposes hands upon him. "Indeed, he does not take part in the council of the clergy, but he accepts assignments and informs the bishop of what is happening. He does not receive the spirit

---

[14] Cyprian, *Ep.* 16, 2; 18, 1; Council of Elvira, can. 32.
[15] Pastor Hermae, *Sim.* 9, 26.
[16] Ibid., 9, 26, 2.

belonging to the *sacerdotium*, in which the presbyters participate, but rather the spirit that is entrusted to him under the bishop's authority" (*Trad. apost.* 8).

The *Catechism of the Catholic Church* (CCC), in the Latin edition (Rome, 1997), no. 875, reserves the term *sacerdotium* for the bishop and presbyter and, using a formulation of Hippolytus, describes the diaconate as *ministerium episcopi*, i.e., as a service to the bishop's representation of the "Priest, Prophet, and Pastor, Jesus Christ" as Head with regard to the Church, which is his Body. This neither calls into question the unity of the "ministerial priesthood", namely that of the sacramental, threefold hierarchy (cf. LG 10), nor does it deny that the deacons in their essential duties participate in the Sacrament of Orders, i.e., in the "ministerial priesthood" at the level of their degree of Order (cf. LG 28–29), and thus "partake in a special way in the mission and grace of the high priest (Christ)" (LG 41). It is clear that the term "*sacerdotium ministeriale seu hierarchicum*" here means not only the degree of the presbyterate, but the threefold *Ordo sacramentalis*, considered primarily from the perspective of the liturgical ministry of sanctification, along with the aspects whereby the prophetic and kingly-pastoral ministry of Christ is actualized. Already at the beginning of the second century, the bishop and martyr Ignatius of Antioch gave expression to the essential interconnections and distinctions among the degrees of Order. "Let everyone revere the deacons as Jesus Christ, the bishop as the image of the Father, and the presbyters as the senate of God and the assembly of the apostles. For without them one cannot speak of the Church."[17]

In the ordination prayer the bishop prays for "the Holy Spirit of grace, of attentiveness and of zeal", so that the candidate may become a deacon in the Church, i.e., "that he may serve God by glorifying God in the liturgy and by his blameless life".[18] Daily prayer with the assembled presbyters and the bishop is one of the deacon's duties.[19]

---

[17] Ignatius, *Trall.* 3, 1; quoted in CCC 1554.
[18] *Trad. apost.* 8; cf. *Const. apost.* 8, 18f.
[19] Ibid. 39.

The developments in theology and in formulations of the faith during the first and second centuries until the time of Hippolytus can serve as a criterion for our theological understanding of the *sacramentum ordinis* in general.

It is certain that there is one *Ordo* that is exercised in three degrees. This Order continues, on a sacramental foundation, the mission and the duties of the apostles in the ministries of the bishop, of the presbyterium, and of the deacons, by virtue of God's will for his Church.[20]

Summarizing the tradition to date, and based on the teaching of the Council of Trent about the Sacrament of Holy Orders as exercised in the priesthood and the diaconate, the *Roman Catechism* describes what the duty of the deacon is. (Note that, in contrast to the subdeacon, the deacon is ordained by the bishop through the laying on of hands.)

> The second Major Order is the Diaconate. It surpasses the Subdiaconate both in its range of function and in its demands of holiness. The Deacon has a special relationship to the bishop; he almost always accompanies him in his official capacity—assisting him at the pulpit, at the altar, and at the administration of the sacraments. The Deacon's distinctive prerogative is to read the Gospel at Mass. In the early Church he often preached; and where there was the custom of having Holy Communion under both species, he administered the Precious Blood. Moreover, he was given the responsibility for the material possessions of the Church, out of which he was to help those in need. The Deacon's office is to be, as it were, the eyes and ears of the bishop. He should be thoroughly acquainted with conditions in the diocese: the level of attendance at Mass, the sacraments and religious instruction.

[20] *Pastor Hermae*, vis. 3, 5, 1; Irenaeus of Lyons, *Haer.* 3, 3, 3; Clement of Alexandria, *Paed.* 3, 12, 97, 2; *Strom.* 6, 107, 2; Origen, *Orat.* 28, 4; Tertullian, *Bapt.* 17, 1; *Fug.* 11, 1; *Mon.* 11, 1; Hippolytus, *Ref.* 9, 12, 22; Cornelius, *Ep. ad Fabian.*; Eusebius, *Histor. eccl.* 6, 43, 11.

On the basis of this information, the bishop should be better able to exhort his people, both privately and publicly. The Deacon also has charge of the lists of catechists and of candidates for the clerical state. Finally, in the absence of bishop and priest, he may preach in church; but not from the regular pulpit (*superiore loco*), so as to indicate that this is not his ordinary function (*proprium munus*).[21]

With regard to the difference between the priest's preaching and that of the deacon, Thomas Aquinas had determined that the deacon preaches only *per modum catechizantis* [as a catechist], while explaining the Gospel as a teacher (*per modum docendi*) is the prerogative of the bishop and the presbyter.[22] The primordial task that Christ entrusted to the bishops to carry out is to proclaim the Gospel as "proprium munus tamquam principalissimum" [their distinctive and foremost duty].[23]

3. The ministry of the *diakonissa/ministra*

From the third century on we can find evidence—in some, though not all regions of the Church—of the development of a specific ecclesial office of service that is conferred upon women in particular.[24] This occurs in connection with the development of additional ministries in the Church, the or-

[21] *The Roman Catechism*, 2, 7, 20.

[22] ST 3, 67, 1 ad 1.

[23] ST 3, 67, 2.

[24] The most comprehensive collection, evaluation, and theological interpretation of all the texts concerning the ecclesial but nonsacramental office of deaconess is presented in Johannes Pinius, *De diaconissarum ordinatione*, in *Acta Sanctorum*, September 1, Antwerp 1746, I–XXVIII. The greater part of the Greek and Latin source texts cited here is reprinted in: Josephine Mayer, *Monumenta de viduis diaconissis virginibusque tractantia* (Bonn, 1938).

dines minores, which are in principle distinct from the apostolic ministry (in the three degrees of bishop, presbyterium, and deacon) that is an essential component of the sacramental nature of the Church.

3.1 *Ecclesial office or degree of sacramental Orders?*

There is an objective distinction between sacramental Order and ecclesial offices; this distinction has been part of the Church's beliefs—as the *Traditio apostolica*, for example, testifies—and it was also set forth by the Second Vatican Council. There is no such thing as an ecclesial office of human origin that participates in some nonsacramental way in the sacramental hierarchy, which consists exclusively of the degrees of bishop, presbyter, and deacon. The apostolate of the laity, on the other hand, consists in a participation in the salvific mission of the Church, but does not share in the mission of the bishop, the presbyter, and the deacon. In addition there is the possibility that lay persons "can be called in different ways to more immediate cooperation in the apostolate of the hierarchy . . . [and be] appointed by the hierarchy to some ecclesiastical offices with a view to a spiritual end" (LG 33).

The offices of deaconess, subdeacon, lector, etc., sometimes are not considered part of the clergy,[25] but sometimes they are.[26] This depends on whether the term "clergy" is meant in the wider or narrower sense, either as the threefold ordained ministry or as a more general grouping of all those who serve in the Church.[27] This is likewise true for the

---

[25] Nicaea, can. 19. *Trad. apost.* 10.

[26] *Const. apost.* 3, 12, 2; 8, 19, 1. Epiphanius of Salamis, *Exp. fidei* 21. Emperor Justinian, *Nov.* 3, 1f.

[27] Acts 1:17; Origen, *In Jer.* 11:3. Jerome, *Ep.* 52, 2.

terms "ministry" and "order", depending on whether it is a question of a sacramental ministry or an ecclesial office, i.e., whether someone is appointed to this or that ministry through *ordination*. In passages where the minor orders and the office of deaconess are counted as part of the clergy, we are dealing, not with a theological statement, but rather with the claim to a livelihood; those who held a significant office could expect financial support from their local church or even from the civil authorities.

Ordo denotes, since the time of Tertullian, (1) the order of God's works in creation, the history of redemption, and providence, (2) the *status religiosus* [religious state] (*Uxor.* 1, 7; *Monog.* 12), (3) the *clergy of the local church*: bishop, presbyter, and deacon, or (4) *promotion to orders* through ordination ["*ordinare*"] (*Cast.* 7; *Monog.* 11f.; *Praes. haer.* 41, 6; Cyprian, *Ep.* 1, 1; 38, 1, etc.). *Ordo* corresponds, practically speaking, to the God-given order of the Old Testament priesthood and its cultic worship, or else to the New Testament order of the apostles and of the arrangements that they made (1 Clement 42, 2; 37, 2) for the installation of bishops and deacons; the term connotes that their mission is derived from Christ "in good order" (*tágma*), as instituted by God for the building up of the Church (1 Cor 12:28, etc.). Since the fourth century, *Ordo* denotes the episcopal degree of ordination (*Cod. Theod.* 16, 5, 26; Dionysius Areopagita, *E. h.* 5; Isidore, *Etymol.*, 7, 12, 3). *Ordinare* can mean both the selection and appointment of a candidate to an office (*katástasis*) (Acts 6:3; Tit 1:5; 1 Clement 42, 4; 43, 1; 44, 2f.; 54, 2) through the laying on of hands, and also the epiclesis with laying on of hands (Gk.: *cheirothesía*; Lat.: *consecratio, benedictio*) by which a bishop, presbyter, or deacon is consecrated. Where "ordination" through the laying on of hands also means, in general, installation in an ecclesial office, deaconesses and the minor orders can be numbered among the *ordo/clerus* (*Const. apost.* 8, 19, 1; Chalcedon, can. 15), without being consecrated as the bishop, presbyter, and deacon are (ibid., 8, 28, 6; Epiphanius, *Haer.* 79, 3). In the twelfth century *Ordo* denotes the ordination ceremony, the [indelible] sacramental character, and the [resulting] spiritual authority (Lombardus, *Sent.* 4, d. 24, c. 13). Because the concept of priesthood became centered upon the presbyteral degree of Holy Orders, a distinction was made between the *ordinatio* of the presbyter and the *consecratio* of the bishop; the difference is one of *dignitas* (*Sent.* IV, d. 24, c. 15). Ever since the renewal of the theology of the episcopal ministry (Vatican II, LG 26), the Sacrament of Holy Orders is described as follows: In the Church there is one *Ordo*, which consists of the *ordines* of bishop, presbyter, and deacon and which is conferred by the bishop through the ordination ceremony as a sacramental consecration (CIC, can. 1008f.).

The redactor of the *Apostolic Constitutions*, in which deaconesses and other ecclesial ministers are numbered among the clergy and are said to be installed in office or "ordained" by a blessing and the laying on of hands, firmly rejects any sort of confusion or blending of the different degrees of ordained ministry. It states that, for bishops, presbyters, and deacons, the different names themselves indicate the distinct duties. If God had wanted an undifferentiated ministry, it could have been communicated in a single consecration. For the sake of order, however, there are different degrees of Order, corresponding to clearly delineated areas of responsibility and competence.[28] Not only the ordained ministry in general, but also its subdivision into bishop, presbyter, and deacon are prescribed by God for the Church.

The Church could not, at her own discretion, declare nonsacramental ecclesial offices to be forms of the *one* ordained ministry, nor could she institute them on her own. The ordained ministry, in its origins, is *one* precisely *in* the three degrees of Order, and not in a way that transcends or abstracts from the order that they designate.

Practically speaking, the difference becomes apparent in the functions that belong specifically to the priesthood: the priest is in charge of proclaiming the Word, exercises the

---

[28] *Const. apost.* 8, 46.

ministries of teaching and governing, and has authority to administer the traditions, especially in connection with the Eucharist. Only from the prescribed duties can we determine the specific meaning of an appointment to sacramental ministry or to an ecclesial office. Thus it is explicitly emphasized that the deaconess, who is equipped for her office with the Holy Spirit through prayer and the laying on of hands, does not perform the functions of the priests and the deacons, but is consecrated to assist with the Baptism of women and to serve the sick and the needy.[29]

Where *"ordinatio"* by the laying on of hands signifies, in general, appointment to various ecclesial offices, the imposition of hands that consecrates must be distinguished from the laying on of hands that is merely a blessing; the former installs (ordains) Christians to the ministry of bishop, presbyter, and deacon, while the latter installs them in an ecclesial office. This objective distinction, which at the time was made deliberately and with theological understanding, was later expressed, in the terminology of a developed sacramental doctrine, as the difference between a tradition and a sacramental, and these terms are perfectly justified. Besides, the lesser value of sacramentals does not so much differentiate them from the traditions; rather, they are bound up with the traditions by the fact that sacramentals, as symbolic actions instituted by the Church, derive their power and meaning from the Church's sacramental mission in the first place.

Besides, it should be noted that the sign of laying on of hands is used in the sacraments of Confirmation and Reconciliation, and also in the blessing of catechumens, for instance.[30] Originally *cheirotonia* had meant the designation of

[29] Ibid. 8, 28, 6; Epiphanius of Salamis, *Haer.* 79, 3; cf. 49, 2. John Chrysostom, *Sac.* 3, 9.
[30] *Trad. apost.* 19.

those who were selected for a ministry and their appoint-ment to it (Acts 14:23; 2 Cor 8:19; *Didache* 15:1). It should be distinguished from the *epithesis ton cheiron* (Acts 6:7; 1 Tim 4:14; 1:18; 2 Tim 1:6) as the communication of the specific ministerial charism.

This distinction, which exists objectively and is present in the Church's understanding, finds its expression in terminol-ogy that increases in precision. In the West, the term *ordinare* has been restricted more and more since the early Middle Ages to the ordination of deacons and presbyters (*consecrare* is used for the bishop); whereas in the East after the fifth cen-tury the technical term for sacramental ordination came to be *cheirotonia*, while *cheirothesia* was reserved for the benediction given in connection with other ecclesial offices (e.g., minor orders).[31]

The result for sacramental theology is quite unambiguous —whether or not this finding happens to be welcome.

In the Catholic [local] churches there was no women's di-

---

[31] On the essential distinction between the laying on of hands as an appointment to an ecclesial office and the consecration that confers the authority of the sacramental Order of bishop, presbyter, or dea-con, cf. Michael Wittig's articles, "Cheirothesia", "Cheirotonia", in LThK 2:1031f.: "In the so-called *Traditio apostolica* [these two terms] are used side by side as synonyms. *Cheirothesia* in the *Apostolic Tradition* is the character that distinguishes the clergyman from the layman; instal-lation [as opposed to ordination] confers those ministries that do not participate in the laying on of hands. . . . The *Apostolic Constitutions* put it differently: Whereas *cheirotonia* is a term reserved for the consecration of bishops, presbyters, deacons, and subdeacons, *cheirothesia* denotes other forms of laying on of hands, for instance at Baptism, with catechumens, or as a rite of reconciliation, etc. Orthodox canon law, following the tradition of Chalcedon (451), uses *cheirothesia* for the lower orders and *cheirotonia* for the higher orders; accordingly, bishops, priests, and dea-cons are ordained to their ministries in the Church through the laying on of hands. In the Eastern tradition the diaconate of women persisted for a long time in the clergy."

aconate corresponding to the diaconal ministry within the threefold *Ordo*. The office of deaconess is clearly distinguished from the office of the deacons. The diaconal ministry was not performed by women as well; rather there was an ecclesial office held only by women, which, admittedly, was usually mentioned before the office of subdeacon in listings of these ecclesial ministries and thus comes to stand at the head of the ecclesial offices (cf. 1 Tim 3:11).[32]

The accusation that the Church Fathers had an antipathy toward the body, women, and sexuality is applicable to the Gnostics instead, whereas an essentially differentiated picture emerges for the Church Fathers.[33] Explaining the "exclusion" of women from the *Ordo sacramentalis* in terms of the Church Fathers' alleged bias, which regarded women as sociologically inferior, is a two-edged argument. After all, the same bishops who introduced the office of the deaconesses as an ecclesial office and repeatedly conferred it upon women are simulta-

---

[32] A pattern that later commentators cited again and again in interpreting 1 Timothy 3:11 is presented by Ambrosiaster, *In 1 Tim.* 3:11. "Because the Apostle addresses women after the deacons, the Cataphrygians seize upon this as an opportunity for heresy and with vain arrogance maintain that the deaconesses, too, must have been ordained; even though they know that the apostles selected seven men as deacons. Could they not find, on that occasion, any suitable woman, since we read that there were holy women with the twelve apostles (cf. Acts 1:14)? . . . Yet the Apostle orders women to be silent in the assembly of the faithful" (Gerhard Ludwig Müller, ed., *Der Empfänger des Weihesakraments: Quellen zur Lehre und Praxis der Kirche, nur Männern das Weihesakrament zu spenden* [Würzburg, 1999], p. 89). See also John Chrysostom, *In 1 Tim. hom.* 11 (PG 62, 555). Epiphanius, *Haer.* 79, 3 (ibid., p. 88). Council of Orange (ibid., p. 98), Synod of Dovin (Armenia): "Women are not permitted to exercise a ministry, except at Baptism" (ibid., p. 109). Isidore of Seville, *De eccl. off.* 2, 18, 11 (ibid., p. 109). *Decretum Gratiani*, cap. 15 (ibid., p. 115). Magister Rufinus, *Summa Decretorum*, causa 27, q. 1 (ibid., p. 320). Robert of Yorkshire, *Liber poenitentialis*, q. 6, 42 (ibid., p. 322). Thomas Aquinas, *In 1 Tim.* 3,11 (ibid., p. 333), etc.

[33] On this subject, see the individual contributions in Enrico Dal Covolo, ed., *Donna e matrimonio alle origine della Chiesa*, Biblioteca di scienze religiose, 122 (Rome, 1996).

neously being accused of misogyny in having suppressed a tradition, dating back to the first few centuries, of sacramental presbyteral and diaconal ministry for women.

3.2 The theological form of an ecclesial office for women

It is extremely significant for ecclesiology, nevertheless, that an ecclesial office for women developed in the first place as a particular expression of the Church's diaconal mission. The full and valid participation of women and men in the Church's universal mission is a consequence of Baptism and is thus an integral part of the Church's self-understanding. Through the working of the Holy Spirit, the baptized person becomes a member of the Church and, cooperating with all sorts of charisms and ministries, contributes to the building up of the Body of Christ.

With regard to sharing fully in salvation, having immediate personal access to God and membership in the Church, there is no distinction between men and women that would be relevant in terms of anthropology or the theology of grace. That is because in Christ we have all become *one*; consequently the Church together with her Head constitutes, as it were, one Person (Gal 3:28). All of this is substantiated by the good news of salvation, which Jesus proclaimed in order to institute these mysteries.

Jesus did not merely criticize the socially accepted role models of his day, which in practice were usually construed to the disadvantage of women in public life, politics, legal matters, and the family. Authoritatively harking back to the will of God in creation, Jesus restored the personal dignity of woman, which is rooted in the image and likeness of God, and made this dignity the measure of a just order for the relations between the sexes in society and the moral criterion with which to evaluate various forms of their intimacy with each other. It is hardly possible, therefore, to explain the fact that Jesus called men only to be members of the Twelve by saying that he was unconsciously dependent upon the spirit of the times or that he was taking into consideration the limited understanding of his disciples. For methodological reasons, the hypothetical argument that if Jesus were alive today he would call women to be apostles is unacceptable. It is impossible to appeal to a hypothetical authority of Jesus on the one hand and on the other hand invalidate his real, historical authority in founding the Church. It is difficult to believe that Jesus, afraid of his own courage "in this matter of great importance, which pertains to the Church's divine constitution" (OS 4), made an exception this one time and set aside his consistent adherence to the will of God, to which he appealed in opposing the casuistry of the Pharisees concerning divorce (Mt 19:8) and on other occasions as well.

The group of people who accompanied him as he proclaimed the Kingdom of God included not only the twelve disciples, but also "some women" who provided for him and his disciples out of their means (Lk 8:3). These women remained faithful to Jesus even to the Cross, while the disciples fled. They form a bridge between Good Friday and Easter Sunday, in that they communicated the Paschal tidings of the empty tomb to the disciples, to whom the glorified Lord then revealed himself as the living, risen Christ and Mediator of the Kingdom of God. The opinion that the only reason the women were not called to be apostles was out of regard for the mentality and legal customs of the time (which viewed women as not qualified to testify in court) is quite widespread and equally foolish. As though God would allow himself to be restricted in his revelation by human legal ordinances, and of such an abstruse sort, to boot!

The question here is not one of juridical qualifications to testify, but rather of bearing witness to the revelation event: that the Crucified One has awakened. The women did in fact become witnesses to this revelation event, in spite of all the legal ordinances of contemporary Judaism. Besides, it is already certain from the Old Testament, and this has never been disputed in the Church's tradition,[34] that women, as prophetesses, have been and can be agents of public revelation (cf. also the patristic discussion of Mary as *prophetissa*) as well as of private revelations.

In Mary, the Mother of the Lord (Lk 1:43) who became the servant of all, we find again a woman who built a bridge between the Incarnation and the public, salvific ministry of Jesus (Gal 4:4–6). At the wedding feast in Cana she points prophetically to Jesus: "Do whatever he tells you" (Jn 2:5), and thereby she testifies as a woman to the Word, which reveals its glory in Jesus; in this way she is a model of faith. Equally significant is the reference in the Gospel of John to Mary, the sister of Lazarus, who anoints Jesus, "the Messiah (which means Christ [the anointed of the Lord])" (Jn 1:41) for his burial and thereby proclaims the salvific meaning of Jesus' death (Jn 12:1–10). Just as Mary will be called blessed by all generations (Lk 1:48) on account of her faith, through which she became the Mother of God, so too throughout the world, wherever the gospel is proclaimed, people will remember the woman who anointed Jesus for his burial and recount what she did (Mk 14:9). Women represent the maternal womb of the Church, in which the life of faith originates and from which the faithful are born as the Body of

---

[34] Thomas Aquinas, ST *Suppl.* 39, 1.

Christ and within which they are sheltered. The Church, the Bride of the Lamb (Rev 19:7; 22:17), symbolized in the person of the Mother of Jesus, the Lamb of God, appears as the Woman, "a *great portent* . . . in heaven" of the Lamb's victory (Rev 12:1; emphasis added).

Worth pondering also is the fact that only in the Catholic Church and in the Orthodox and ancient Oriental Churches, which have never known women in apostolic ministry, do we find [1] that the feminine symbolism for the creaturely status of man, for faith, grace, and the Church, has been developed as nowhere else in the Christian world, and also [2] a great esteem for the services rendered to the Church by women in religious communities and for the sacramental foundation of motherhood in the Christian family, and last but not least [3] a vivid awareness that God allowed the Incarnation of his Eternal Word to depend upon the faith response of a woman who, as Irenaeus of Lyons says, by her obedience became the *causa salutis*[35] for herself and for the whole human race, inasmuch as we receive grace through faith.

Women and the feminine dimension of mankind's relationship to God, which they represent, are essential elements of the Church's very being and mission. Together with the twelve apostles, these women—Mary, the Mother of Jesus, and his relatives (Acts 1:14)—form the nucleus of the primordial Church of Jerusalem and thus present the archetype and model for the Church in every age.

Especially in the Pauline communities we meet many women who render many forms of service and assistance to the Apostle or to the communities; thus they, too, perform apostolic activity in the wider sense (Rom 16:6). In

---

[35] Irenaeus of Lyons, *Haer.* 3, 22, 4.

the context of the charismatic development of the Church, women who have converted to the faith receive the charisms of prophetic speech (1 Cor 11:5) and of service (Rom 12:4) just as men do. Paul and the communities in the Pauline tradition (1 Cor 14:33–40; 1 Tim 2:11) do not seem to have felt that the prohibition against women teaching in the assembly (which is said to rest upon the authority of Christ and of the Apostle) is in conflict with prophetic speech or with the charism of service. We are dealing in the latter instance with a Spirit-filled witness within the assembled community to one's personal faith in Christ (1 Cor 14:16, 37), and in the former instance with the official proclamation of the Word and of Christian doctrine, which is entrusted to the presbyters (as presiders) and to the bishops (pastors) (1 Tim 5:17; 3:5).

Inasmuch as *service* [*diakonia*] is the expression of the radical change of heart whereby Christians are to be conformed to the service of Christ and his submission to the will of the Father (Phil 2:6–11), the demand that a Christian wife serve her husband submissively is more understandable, at least within the parameters of a mutual subjection in their common reverence for Christ (Eph 5:21), who loved the Church and gave himself up for her—thereby giving an example for husbands of a loving attitude which is essential to marriage (Eph 5:24f.). It must be made clear that this is not just theological embroidering upon social structures; rather such structures, to the extent that they are opposed to the personal dignity of man and woman, have to be dismantled and overcome through Christian witness.

As mothers, women ought to be witnesses to the faith with regard to their children (1 Tim 2:15). Indeed, a woman who is a believer sanctifies her unbelieving husband (1 Cor 7:14). In handing on the faith they become, as it were, nurseries of apostolic vocations, like Timothy's grandmother Lois and his mother Eunice (2 Tim 1:5). St. Paul sends greetings to the mother of Rufus, because she became his, the Apostle's, mother as well (Rom 16:13; cf. Mk 3:35).

Various forms of "diaconal" support for the Apostle and the Christian communities were bundled together here and there in the services rendered by individual women and to some extent became institutionalized into a "ministry" or an office. Thus Paul commends "our sister Phoebe, a deaconess (*he diakonos*) of the church at Cenchreae" (Rom 16:1). Even though the masculine form of the word *diakonos* is used, one cannot conclude that Paul is using the ministerial title of "deacon" here, since in this context *diakonos* still means "servant" in general, and the feminine form is indicated, not by a feminine ending, but by a feminine article. Not until the third century do we find the specifically Christian neologism "*diaconissa*", which appears in Latin also as "*diacona*". The use here of the formula, "a deaconess/servant of the church at Cenchreae" refers to a particular sort of helpful activity that Phoebe took charge of. In a letter by the [second-century] governor of Bithynia, Pliny the Younger, two women are mentioned who are described as "*ministrae*" among the Christians (10, 96f.); it is not possible, however, to determine anything further about the theological significance of this title, and we certainly cannot conclude that this office had a sacramental character.

Some exegetes speculate about whether the women mentioned in the passage about deacons in the First Letter to Timothy are not the wives of deacons, but rather women who have diaconal duties (1 Tim 3:11). Nothing in particular is said about the duties of these women. Instructional and leadership activities were certainly not included, as we can infer from the prohibition against women teaching or governing found in the same letter (cf. 1 Tim 2:11f.). Especially in the case of the enrolled widows, who are mentioned in the pastoral letters, one can suppose that women served in a certain official capacity in the community. A woman should be "enrolled" as a widow only if she is "well attested for her good deeds, as one who has brought up children, shown hospitality, washed the feet of the saints [cf. Jn 13:14], relieved the afflicted, and devoted herself to doing good in every way" (1 Tim 5:9–10).

Here we find the beginnings of a special ecclesiastical state for widows, which through prayer and example in the area of *diakonia* contributes much toward building up the Church spiritually.[36] Ignatius associates the widowed state with the virgins[37] and suggests a gradual development, at the end of which the diaconal duties of the enrolled widows are performed by the consecrated virgins, upon whom the office of deaconess is conferred. Thus the deaconess is often the superior of a cloistered community of religious women, as Gregory of Nyssa and others testify.[38] A line of development leads from deaconesses to abbesses. It can be determined, furthermore, that abbesses, in spite of many claims to the contrary, never exercised episcopal jurisdiction—not because they were women, but rather because a bishop's jurisdiction is rooted in the episcopal degree of Holy Orders.

A woman is admitted to the widowed state only after having been tested. She is elected and installed through the Word and appointed to serve the community by her prayers, in contrast to the clergy, which in the writings of Hippolytus is restricted to the bishop, presbyters, and deacons.[39]

[36] Polycarp, *2 Phil.* 4, 3.
[37] Ignatius, *Smyrn.* 13, 1.
[38] *Vita Macrinae*, BKV 56, 360.
[39] *Trad. apost.* 10.

In the *Apostolic Constitutions* (a collection of older Church ordinances compiled around 380) a prayer for consecrating deaconesses is recorded. It should be kept in mind, however, that this document is in no way representative for the entire Church of this period and had not been received as authoritative [*rezipiert*] in its entirety either, but only individual parts of it, which came from earlier sources and were considered to be indubitably Catholic. According to the *Apostolic Constitutions*, the bishop, assisted by the presbyter, deacon, and the other deaconesses, places his hands upon the deaconess [candidate] and prays:

> O Eternal God, the Father of our Lord Jesus Christ, the Creator of man and of woman, who didst replenish with the Spirit Miriam, and Deborah, and Anna, and Huldah; who didst not disdain that Thy only begotten Son should be born of a woman; who also in the tabernacle of the testimony, and in the temple, didst [appoint] women to be keepers of Thy holy gates; do Thou now also look down upon this Thy servant, who [has been elected] to the office of a deaconess, and grant her Thy Holy Spirit, and cleanse her from all filthiness of flesh and spirit, that she may worthily discharge the work which is committed to her to Thy glory, and the praise of Thy Christ, with whom glory and adoration be to Thee and the Holy Spirit for ever. Amen.[40]

In the ranking of the ministries, the deaconess is listed after the bishop, the presbyters, and the deacons and before the subdeacon, the lectors, and the singers; about her responsibilities it says: "A deaconess does not bless, nor perform anything belonging to the office of presbyters or deacons, but only is to keep the doors, and to minister to the presbyters in the baptizing of women, on account of decency."[41]

[40] *Const. apost.* 8, 19f.
[41] Ibid., 8, 28.

In the High Middle Ages, when the sacramentality of Holy Orders was elaborated within the framework of general sacramental theology, the sacramental character of the individual degrees of Order was measured by the sacramental functions of the recipient. Since the deaconess does not perform the functions of the deacon, whose degree was clearly reckoned among the holy orders and thus as part of the actual sacrament, her consecration is not a sacramental promotion to the diaconate. Thus Thomas Aquinas says:

> The other sacraments are given that certain effects may be received. . . . Hence it behoves the sacrament of Order to be differentiated according to the diversity of acts. . . . Hence the distinction of Orders is derived from their relation to the Eucharist. For the power of Order is directed either to the consecration of the Eucharist itself, or to some ministry in connexion with this sacrament of the Eucharist. . . . The co-operation of the ministers is directed either to the sacrament itself, or to the recipients. If the former, this happens in three ways. For in the first place there is the ministry whereby the minister co-operates with the priest in the sacrament itself, by dispensing, but not by consecrating, for this is done by the priest alone; and this belongs to the deacon.[42]

With respect to the deaconess, Thomas summarizes the valid teaching of the Church. The male sex is a requirement for receiving the Orders of the presbyterate (*sacerdotium*) and the diaconate, not only *de necessitate praecepti*, but also *de necessitate sacramenti*. The deaconess and the *presbytera* are not women who held the office of deacon and presbyter: "But *deaconess* there [in the *Decretals*] denotes a woman who shares in some act of a deacon, namely who reads the homilies in

---

[42] Thomas Aquinas, ST *Suppl.* 37, 1 and 2; cf. Peter Lombard, *Sent.* 4, 24, 10; Gratian, *Decretum*, p. 1, d. 25, can. 1: Friedberg 1:90.

the Church; and *priestess* (*presbytera*) means a widow, for the
word *presbyter* means elder."[43]

The gradual disappearance of the office of deaconess[44]

[43] *Suppl.* 39, 1.

[44] Cf. the brief overview of the history and theology of deaconesses
by Eva-Maria Faber, article "Diakon, Historisch-theologisch", in LThK
3:179–81, at 180f.: "There is evidence for the existence of deaconesses
in the East (besides Egypt and Ethiopia) from the third to the tenth centuries, and in the West from the sixth until the thirteenth century; their
status, however, can hardly be compared with the ministry of the deacon. . . . The difference between the women's and the men's diaconate
is evident also at the initiation of the diaconate. For the women one
usually speaks of blessing or consecration and not of ordination; where
an ordination with the imposition of hands does take place (as in the
case of the subdeacon and lector, too), it is distinguished in numerous
ways from that of the male deacon. . . . On the basis of these historical
findings, an attempt to create a ministry of deaconesses today would in
fact institute a new practice, which would have no connection to any
unified, continuous tradition." This conclusion also receives historical
and theological confirmation in M. B. von Stritzky, "Der Dienst der
Frau in der Alten Kirche", in LJ 28 (1978): 136–54. Special reference
should be made here to the comprehensive study (unfortunately not
acknowledged in German-speaking territories) by Aimé Georges Martimort, *Deaconesses: An Historical Study*, trans. by K. D. Whitehead (San
Francisco: Ignatius Press, 1986). The attempt of A. A. Thiermeyer, "Der
Diakonat der Frau", ThQ 173 (1993): 226–36 to reinterpret the historical findings in the direction of a sacramental diaconal ministry must be
deemed a failure. Cf. Hans Jorissen, "Theologische Bedenken gegen die
Diakonatsweihe von Frauen", in Peter Hünermann, Albert Biesinger,
Marianne Heimbach-Steins, Anne Jensen, eds., *Diakonat: Ein Amt für
Frauen in der Kirche—Ein frauengerechtes Amt* (Ostfildern, 1997), pp. 86–
97, citation at p. 94: "The ministry of the deaconess presents itself in
historical retrospect as an extremely complex phenomenon that varies
widely depending on geographic region and time period. A continuity of
tradition is lacking. Even in passages where the ordination of deaconesses
with the imposition of hands and an epiclesis is structured analogously
to the ordination of a deacon, e.g., in the *Apostolic Constitutions* and especially in the later Byzantine Rite, the historical evidence does not permit
us to speak of an equality of rank between the two ordinations. Martimort correctly concludes, 'However great the solemnity surrounding
the ceremony and the external similarity with the ordination of a deacon

even in the Eastern Churches—in the West it was scarcely known and even met with resistance—probably should not be chalked up to discrimination against women, but can also be explained by the trend that left fewer and fewer functions to be performed by the so-called *ordines minores*. The office did live on in other forms, however, in the numerous contemplative and active religious orders, and it found new expression in the congregations devoted to teaching. Under other titles, the institutionalized, official participation of women in the apostolate of the Universal Church in *martyria, leiturgia*, and *diakonia* (witness, liturgy, and service; cf. LG 33) resulted in decisive contributions to the life of the Church in the modern world long before there was any talk about restoring the office of deaconess.

Diametrically opposed to the spirit of membership in Christ and to the significance of the ordained ministries and the ecclesial offices is the perspective that aspires to ministry as a way of sharing in the so-called "power", or carries out these ministries, with respect to the faithful in one's charge,

---

may have been, the Byzantine deaconess is still not a deacon; it is an entirely different ministry.' Especially noteworthy is the explicit exclusion of the deaconess from any liturgical service at the altar, from the public exercise of the ministry of proclamation, and from the solemn administration of Baptism. 'The reasons for this lie (unambiguously) in the exclusion of women from the ministerial priesthood.' The men's diaconate and the women's diaconate in the ancient Church are not two equivalent branches of one diaconal ministry. There is *no* historic support for the sacramentality (in the current dogmatic understanding of the term) of an independent diaconate *without an intrinsic reference* to the episcopal-presbyteral ministry, resulting from diaconal ordination; and there are good reasons for this. As the research conference [*Studientagung*] of German-speaking liturgists in 1978 determined, history provides 'no solid basis' for a sacramental diaconate of women. Accordingly the historical arguments of the Würzburg Synod, to the extent that they appeal to the deaconesses in the Church of antiquity, must be corrected."

as a way of catering to one's personal appetites for influence, prestige, and the power of those who want to "have the say".

You could scarcely find a better exposition of Romans 16:1, the biblical passage where for the first time a woman is mentioned in a special ministry of service to the community, than in Origen's commentary on the Letter to the Romans:

> The passage teaches with apostolic authority that women, too, can be appointed to the *ministerium* of the Church. This Phoebe, who has an office (*officium*) in the church of Cenchreae, is mentioned by Paul with great praise. . . . Thus the God-fearing Phoebe, who assists and serves everyone, is permitted to assist and serve even the Apostle. Hence the passage teaches two things: that there were women also who ministered to the community, . . . and that such women should be accepted into ministry who had assisted many and by their good offices had won the Apostle's praise. The Apostle also reminds [his readers] that the brethren ought to honor those who devote themselves to good works in the community and reward their activity. Wherever their service is needed, even in worldly matters, they should be held in honor.[45]

4. Summary and conclusion

Summing up the conclusive results of the historical development of the diaconate using theological criteria, the Second Vatican Council offers a fundamental declaration about the divine institution of the *one* hierarchical, i.e., sacramental ministry in the various Orders of the bishop, the presbyters, and the deacons, as it has become impressed upon and clearly

[45] *In Rom.* 10, 17.

defined in the sacramental economy of the Church under the guidance of the Spirit (LG 18; 28).

The ministry of the deacon, too, has a sacramental basis, through which it is associated in the one *Ordo* with the bishop and springs from the same root of apostolic ministry, whereby Jesus gives men a share in his own mission from the Father and has entrusted to them the exercise of his saving ministry *in* the Church and *for* the world.

Sacramental ordination is not a privilege whereby one Christian can exalt himself over others. Rather, it creates a personal relation to Christ by virtue of a vocation, mission, and authorization, so that the ordained man, by a *configuratio cum Christo*, is able to act, in the person of Christ as Head of the Church, within the Church and upon the Church as the Body of Christ (cf. PO 2; LG 20). This personal relation is the center of the theology and spirituality of this ministry, in which his various duties are also integrated. These duties therefore cannot be distributed among various nonsacramental ministries. Although historically there was occasionally a blurring of boundaries between his individual duties and the presbyteral ministry, it is still clear, from an overall perspective, that the deacon can function in all areas of the Church's mission: in the proclamation of the Word, the liturgy, and the *diakonia* of charitable service and its special ministry, in each instance with a particular emphasis but, it should be noted, in a diaconal and not a presbyteral manner.

He does this in the manner given to him specifically in ordination: that of the *ministerium*, not of the *sacerdotium*. By no means does the deacon perform functions that normally any layman performs in actualizing the common priesthood and the diaconal mission of the Church. Even though in an emergency any layman can carry out the duties with which the deacon is charged, that does not allow us to regard the diaconate as an afterthought, a bundle of lay ministries, or to misconstrue diaconal ordination as a secondary justification of the same. For the diaconate is one of those "functions which are so extremely necessary for the life of the Church" (LG 29) and thus constitutes an essential component of the *sacramentum ordinis* instituted by God for the Church. It is not one of those ecclesial offices to which individual believers, by reason of the specifically lay apostolate, can be "called in different ways to more immediate cooperation in the apostolate of the hierarchy" (LG 33). It is said of the *sacramentum ordinis* as a whole that the hierarchical priesthood differs from the common priesthood of all the faithful, not in degree, but essentially; therefore with regard to the diaconal ministry in particular it can be concluded that, being part of the Sacrament of Holy Orders, it differs essentially and not only in degree from lay ministries and ecclesial offices for laymen (LG 10).

The sacramental character, rather, is the source of the deacon's functions. Ordination is a dynamic and fundamental event, from which the diaconal duties proceed as a specific representation of the service that Christ renders to his Church—the Head to the Body. Thus *Lumen gentium* derives the duties of the deacon, which cannot be listed here exhaustively, from the sacramental grace through which the deacons "are dedicated to the People of God, in conjunction with the bishop and his body of priests, in the service of the liturgy, of the Gospel and of works of charity" (LG 29).

In their person and in their sacramental ministry, they make the *diakonia* of Jesus Christ and God's selfless love for the world tangible and audible, and this should be the standard and the heart of Christian life for every individual Christian, for the Church as a whole, and for the pastoral ministry of her bishops and the presbyters.

As a sacramental ministry, the diaconate is an effective,

i.e., Church-edifying sign of the radical novelty of the relation between God and man in Jesus Christ, who "came not to be served but to serve, and to give his life as a ransom for many" (Mk 10:45).

The diaconal ministry has all of the characteristics of the Sacrament of Holy Orders: originating in the salvific mission and will of Christ for the Church; sustained by his abiding efficacy as the glorified Lord in the Spirit; connected with the mission of the apostles through the imposition of hands by the bishop (cf. 1 Tim 4:14; 2 Tim 1:6; Acts 6:6); conferring the Holy Spirit and grace, which makes the recipient a suitable minister of Christ (DH 1326); ordained in an unrepeatable way (*character indelebilis*), with the specific ministerial responsibilities designated in the ordination prayer (DH 1765f., 1773, 3860; LG 29). In his "functions which are so extremely necessary for the life of the Church", the deacon serves "the People of God, in conjunction with the bishop and his body of priests, in the service of the liturgy, of the Gospel and of works of charity" (LG 29; CD 15). In representing Christ, he has the following ministerial duties (*officia*): directing the charitable works of the Church, administration, conferring solemn Baptism, distributing the Eucharist, reading Sacred Scripture to the faithful, conducting liturgies of the Word and of prayer for the faithful (LG 29), and, in certain circumstances, even "governing scattered Christian communities in the name of the bishop or parish priest" (AG 16). Historically there is some blurring in the boundaries between diaconal and presbyteral functions (e.g., confession to a deacon in an emergency), just as since the Second Vatican Council and to this day there has been discussion about the exact, specific form of the diaconal ministry.[46] According to systematic theology, in any

---

[46] Of the recent literature, special attention should be given to: Al-

case, the deacon receives a sacramental ordination, and the diaconate is part of the Church's *Ordo*.[47] His ordination does not signify the recognition of lay ministries already being carried out. Where the ministries pertaining to the deacon *ex ratione sacramenti* are in fact being carried out by laymen, ordination is advisable, because these functions are rooted in the sacramental character of the diaconate (cf. AG 16).

> Strengthened by sacramental grace they are dedicated to the People of God, in conjunction with the bishop and his body of priests, in the service of the liturgy, of the Gospel and of works of charity. It pertains to the office of a deacon, in so far as it may be assigned to him by the competent authority, to administer Baptism solemnly, to be custodian and distributor of the Eucharist, in the name of the Church, to assist at and to bless marriages, to bring Viaticum to the dying, to read the sacred scripture to the faithful, to instruct and exhort the people, to preside over the worship and the prayer of the faithful, to administer sacramentals, and to officiate at funeral and burial services. Dedicated to works of charity and functions of administration, deacons should recall the admonition of St. Polycarp: "Let them be merciful, and zealous, and let them walk according to the truth of the Lord, who became the servant of all" (*Ad Phil.* 5, 2). (LG 29)

phonse Borras and Bernard Pottier, *La Grâce du diaconat: Questions actuelles autour du diaconat latin* (Brussels, 1998).

[47] See Congregation for Catholic Education, *Ratio fundamentalis institutionis diaconorum permanentium* [Directory for the ministry and life of permanent deacons] (Libreria editrice Vaticana, 1998).

ACKNOWLEDGMENTS

Acknowledgment of previously published material

I. "A Challenge for Contemporary Ecclesiology" = "*Frauen sind Kirche*", foreword to Gerhard Ludwig Müller, ed., *Frauen in der Kirche: Eigensein und Mitverantwortung* (Würzburg, 1999), pp. 7–20 (expanded).

II. "Who Receives the Sacrament of Holy Orders in the Degrees of Priesthood and Diaconate?" = "*Wer empfängt das Weihesakrament in den Stufen des Priestertums und des Diakonats?*", introduction to Gerhard Ludwig Müller, ed., *Der Empfänger des Weihesakraments: Quellen zu Lehre und Praxis der Kirche, nur Männern das Weihesakrament zu spenden* (Würzburg, 1999), pp. 21–32. Expanded in particular with: "*Die entscheidende Frage nicht geklärt: Zu der Studie Dorothea Reiningers über den Diakonat der Frau*", by Gerhard Ludwig Müller, in *Die Tagespost*, November 6, 1999, p. 13.

III. "Priesthood: Is a Baptized Man the Only Possible Valid Recipient of Holy Orders?" = "*Priestertum: Kann nur der getaufte Mann gültig das Weihesakrament empfangen? Zur Lehrentscheidung in 'Ordinatio sacerdotalis'*", in G. L. Müller, *Frauen in der Kirche*, pp. 278–356 (slightly revised).

IV. "The Sacramental Diaconate" = "*Der sakramentale Diakonat: Geschichtliche Entfaltung—systematische Perspektiven*", in *Archiv für katholisches Kirchenrecht* 166 (1997): 43–68 (expanded).

SCRIPTURE INDEX

SUBJECT INDEX

abbesses, 137, 161n82, 217
Achiacus, 191
Aërius of Sebaste, 143n45
Ambrose, 51–52, 103n13, 127n29, 168n94
Ambrosiaster, 155, 210n32
Andronicus, 119
anthropology of men and women
  Aquinas on, 173–74
  corporeality, 25, 81, 95–98, 108–9, 111
  equal dignity, 25, 31–33, 41–42, 75, 81–84, 112n17, 114, 166–68
  gender differences (*See* gender)
  theological, 76–78, 98, 110–11, 114, 169
Apollos, 119, 146, 153, 190
apostles, 117–24, 139–41, 150–51, 162
Aquila, 149
Aquinas, Thomas
  on Holy Orders, 47, 56, 64n2, 172–74
  theological reasons for reserving to men, 160–75, 204, 213, 219
Archippus, 190
Augustine, 111n17, 170–71

Baptism, 105, 115, 161n82, 167, 167n94, 173, 210
Barnabas, 119, 123
Basnage, Jacques, 51
Beauvoir, Simone de, 26, 167
belief implied by practice, 65, 68, 139–40, 176, 177n112
bishops
  office of, 46, 89, 121–22, 124–25, 130, 142–45, 186–87, 204
  representing Christ, 121, 121n20, 126–28, 202
blessings structure, 47–50, 57, 149–50, 220n44
  See also nonsacramental consecration
Bonaventure, 163–65
Bride/Bridegroom symbolism, 33, 98, 107–13, 109n16, 113–17, 164

Canon Law, Code of, 43, 159
Cataphrygians, 151, 155, 210n32
Catholic Church
  authority, 20–32, 35–37, 87–89, 124, 131–35
  belief implied by practice, 65, 68, 139–40, 176, 177n112
  as the Bride of Christ, 113–16 (*See also* symbolism)

237

reserved to men, 35n1, 105, 107–13, 136–40, 150–59, 164, 174, 204, 210n32, 213, 219

nature of, 31–33, 38–40, 49–52, 63–79, 90–91, 111–13, 125–30, 178–81, 221–23

unity of *Ordo*, 45–47, 50, 142–43, 192, 198–99, 202–3, 210, 222–23, 226

Hünermann, Peter, 38, 50–51, 54, 82n9, 83n

Ignatius of Antioch
on enrolled widows, 217
on structure of Holy Orders, 135, 135n39, 142
on symbolism of clergy, 132n34, 135, 135n39, 197–200, 202

imposition of hands. *See* laying on of hands

infallibility, 78

"in his image and likeness", 25, 97–98, 101–5, 111, 111n17, 114, 166, 211

Innocent III, 158

Innocent IV, 158

institutional will of Christ, 66–67, 70, 77, 86–87, 139, 141, 162–63, 172, 176

International Theological Congress (Stuttgart, 1997), 54

Irenaeus of Lyons, 29

James, 123

Jerome, 157

Jesus Christ
as bishop archetype, 121, 121n20, 126–28, 202
bridegroom symbolism and, 33, 98, 107–13, 109n16, 113–17, 164
as deacon archetype, 183–87, 192, 197–200, 202, 224–25
foundational intention of, 66–67, 70, 77, 86–87, 139, 141, 162–63, 172, 176
as model for relationships, 32, 111–14, 117
as priest archetype, 63, 95–96, 106–13, 127n29, 132, 132n34, 164

Johannes Pinius, 56, 204n24

John Damascene, 157

John Paul II, 19, 35–36, 36n1, 63, 159–60

Josephus Flavius, 123

Junia/Junias, 119

Justin Martyr, 52, 123, 135n40

Justin (philosopher), 200

Kant, Immanuel, 80

Karpokrates, 154n59

laity/clergy distinction, 33, 38–40, 90–91, 113, 125–30, 221–23

laying on of hands
as consecration/blessing, 56–57, 149–50, 195–96, 203, 208–9, 209n31, 220n44
in ordination, 124–25, 130, 138–39, 147, 195–96, 200–201, 206, 208–9